YOU ARE MORE THAN A TYPE
EMBRACING WHOLENESS WITH THE ENNEAGRAM OF ESSENCE

TAMMY HENDRIX, LCSW

Enneagram of
ESSENCE

Copyright © 2023 by Tammy Hendrix, LCSW

All rights reserved. No part of this publication may be reproduced, distributed, or transmitted in any form or by any means, including photocopying, recording, or other electronic or mechanical methods, without the prior written permission of the publisher, except in the case of brief quotations embodied in critical reviews and certain other noncommercial uses permitted by copyright law.

ISBN: 979-8-218-33102-3

For more information, email hendrixtammy@gmail.com

Disclaimer

The case studies and client examples presented in this book are based on real-life interactions from my private practice. In order to protect the privacy and confidentiality of the individuals involved, all names have been changed. Furthermore, specific identifying details have been modified or omitted to further ensure anonymity. Any resemblance to actual persons, living or dead, or to actual events or locales is purely coincidental. The intention behind sharing these examples is solely to provide insight into the Enneagram and its applications, without violating the trust or privacy of any individual.

*To my first Enneagram teacher and guide, my mother. And, to all the visionaries who cultivate this wisdom—past, present, **and future.***

CONTENTS

Free Gift	1
Foreword	3
Introduction	5

FOUNDATION

Origins, Essence, & Personality	11
Three Centers & Directions	16
Wholeness & Embodiment	24
Reading Guide	29

YOUR HEAD CENTER

Sanctuary of Your Mind	35
Type 7—Freedom	42
Type 6—Trust	67
Type 5—Clarity	94

YOUR HEART CENTER

Haven of Your Heart	123
Type 4—Belonging	130
Type 3—Value	154
Type 2—Compassion	179

YOUR GUT CENTER

Ground of Your Being	209
Type 1—Integrity	216
Type 9—Harmony	241
Type 8—Strength	268

INTEGRATION

INTEGRATION	295
Acknowledgments	299
About the Author	303
A Request	305

FREE GIFT

I am delighted to offer an exclusive gift—**a beautiful, colorful PDF download** of the Enneagram symbol, enriched with the nine essences.

Your Companion for Deeper Enneagram Exploration

This gift isn't just aesthetically pleasing, it's a guide to the nourishing essences of the nine Enneagram types. Use it as a daily inspiration in your journey towards understanding and embracing the wholeness and nourishing essence of your being.

ACCESS YOUR FREE GIFT HERE:

https://mailchi.mp/5a984a41ca0b/freegift

FOREWORD

Many decades ago, when the Enneagram was just emerging from the shadows, I started a journey that would shape the course of my life. Guided by ancient wisdom, I sought to understand the depths of who and what we truly are.

Today, I see that same passion mirrored in Tammy's eyes and etched across every page of this inspiring book.

I have the unusual grace to journey alongside Tammy, who is my daughter, as she discovers wholeness by embracing the nine facets of her being and the essence that our three centers bestow—universal wisdom, love, and power.

Reading through her introductory chapter transported me back to those humid mornings, where we'd engage in profound conversations about the Enneagram, often accompanied by a cup of tea and mutual curiosity. Seeing my own daughter not just take an interest in, but passionately evolve my teachings and make them her own has been one of the most fulfilling experiences of my life.

This isn't your typical Enneagram book. It's a deeply therapeutic, mystical, and holistic dive into the depth of the Enneagram.

FOREWORD

With stories that resonate, insights that captivate, and exercises that transform, Tammy has crafted a manual for all who seek to understand not just their essence, but the universality of human experience.

As I've often told Tammy, the Enneagram isn't about putting ourselves into boxes but breaking free from them. By emphasizing the importance of recognizing and embracing all nine types within, she offers a fresh perspective—one that champions integration over division and wholeness over fragmentation.

In the pages ahead, you will not only discover the Enneagram's wisdom but also the warmth of a shared journey.

I invite you, dear reader, to journey with my daughter. Allow her insights, stories, and exercises to be your guide. As you traverse each page, remember that this isn't just about a system of understanding, but about embracing the richness of our multifaceted being and discovering our shared truth.

Lissa Friedman, PhD
Founder of—
The Enneagram Embodiment Tradition
The Enneagram School of Awakening

INTRODUCTION

WELCOME TO THE ENNEAGRAM OF ESSENCE

Has the Enneagram ever led you to feel...

- Overwhelmed or confused?
- Embarrassed or misunderstood?
- Uncertain about fitting neatly into any one type?

If you're nodding, take comfort—you're in good company. Many are drawn to the Enneagram journey seeking clarity and hope, only to feel confused by its complexity or discouraged by negative portrayals of the types.

That's why I wrote this book.

I wanted to offer a relatable, invigorating, and truly holistic perspective on the Enneagram. My goal was to balance the practical and the profound, providing insights that not only deepen understanding but also offer tangible, real-world applications.

Central to my approach is a focus on the essence of each Enneagram type. This approach fosters not just compassion, but also inspiration and affection for each type. By engaging deeply with the sensory

INTRODUCTION

aspects of each type's essence, the Enneagram becomes more than a tool for analysis. It elevates into a transformative guide for meaningful personal growth.

Dive into this book and...

- Emerge with a clarity *you can feel.*
- Engage with insights that *uplift and empower.*
- Discover descriptions that resonate through *your whole being.*
- Experience practices that soothe fixations and *anchor you in wholeness.*

This journey offers three key objectives:

1. Deepen your understanding of your primary type.
2. Discover that all nine types reside within you.
3. Embrace the nourishing essence of each type.

Over twenty years as an Enneagram educator and therapist, I've gathered a wealth of insights and therapeutic gems. From this rich experience, I have honed clear, actionable steps to navigate the Enneagram of Personality *and Essence.*

Woven into these teachings, you'll find my personal stories, where I reveal how each Enneagram type has illuminated a facet of myself.

My goal? To inspire you to discover your own facets.

Are you ready for a glimpse? I'll start by sharing the transformative time that first drew me to the Enneagram.

THAT TIME I HEARD THE ENNEAGRAM'S CALL

For over two decades, I've been on a remarkable journey with

INTRODUCTION

the Enneagram—a path that began before I even knew it would call upon me.

I was around twenty years old when I first stumbled upon my mother's well-read Enneagram books, filled with hand-scribbled notes and reflections. They were displayed on shelves that welcomed guests at the entrance of her home—as if calling to me each time I entered.

My mother, a visionary who studied with the original legends of the Enneagram, founded the Embodiment Tradition—a visceral approach that piqued my interest. Her influence was a light that drew me to the mystical world of the Enneagram.

On a steamy Florida morning, I had the opportunity to attend one of her day-long Enneagram workshops. It was a whirlwind of insights, exercises, and profound connections. I found myself drawn into this intricate realm, feeling both challenged and enchanted by its complexity.

That summer workshop marked not just an introduction but a portal into a transformative journey. Those ancient symbols and concepts took hold of my heart, igniting a lifelong passion.

I went on to study with many Enneagram teachers during the 2000s, delving into various perspectives. As I immersed deeper into the traditional approach to the Enneagram of Personality over the years, a restlessness grew within me—a yearning for something more nurturing, more holistic, more real.

This inspired me to evolve the Enneagram beyond insight, into a practical guide—emphasizing wholeness and healing through essence. As a somatic psychotherapist I already had a wealth of resources to explore healing beyond cognitive analysis. Somatic

INTRODUCTION

therapy techniques emphasize bodily sensations, nurturing nervous system awareness and wellness.

Inner, somatic awareness is vital for connecting to the essence of the types.

This book offers a practical approach to the profound wisdom of the Enneagram, integrating ancient insights with modern somatic psychology. And it all began with that time I heard the call of the Enneagram, ignited by my mother's passion as I set forth on a path all my own.

A journey that I now invite you to explore.
Ready to embrace your wholeness?

FOUNDATION

ORIGINS, ESSENCE, & PERSONALITY

ORIGINS

With roots that can be traced back over a millennium to ancient traditions, including Sufism and early Christian mysticism, the Enneagram has a rich, yet somewhat mysterious, historical lineage.

Today, it serves as a multifaceted map of both the human psyche and the nourishing qualities of inner essence.

The Enneagram symbol gained modern attention in the early 20th century through the work of Russian mystical philosopher George Gurdjieff. He regarded it as a symbol of sacred mathematics and geometry—depicting cosmic laws and the interconnectedness of the universe.

The system as we recognize it today, especially the Enneagram of Personality, primarily took shape in the latter half of the 20th century. Significant contributions came from South American spiritual and psychological scholars, Oscar Ichazo and Claudio Naranjo.

It is now applied in many modern contexts—from personal growth and therapy to organizational development.

ORIGINS, ESSENCE, & PERSONALITY

The Enneagram's iconic nine-pointed star symbolizes nine unique patterns, each with its own core motivation, behaviors, defense mechanisms, and underlying essence—offering an energetic distinct to each type.

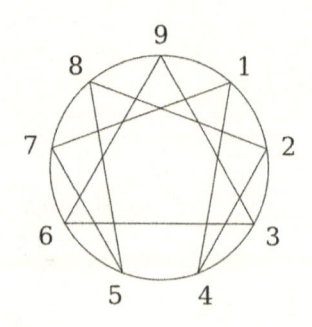

QUALITIES OF YOUR ESSENCE

This book focuses on the nine unique qualities of essence—inner resources at the core of the types. Understanding the essence of the Enneagram types is key to utilizing it as a practical guide for growth.

Essence is your authentic nature—an inner experience and sense of self that goes deeper than the limits of personality traits. Although you can not measure essence, you can certainly feel its nourishing effects.

The Enneagram is structured into three centers: Head, Heart, and Gut, each of which carries a core essence—wisdom, love, and power, respectively.

Each of these centers is further organized into three specific types, which add nuance to their core essence. This results in nine distinct but interconnected facets of essence—nine qualities of inner nourishment.

In this book, I use multiple terms to describe the essence of each type—offering different perspectives that might resonate with you.

ORIGINS, ESSENCE, & PERSONALITY

QUICK GUIDE TO ENNEAGRAM ESSENCE

Head Center: Wisdom

- **Type 7:** Joy, Freedom, Abundance
- **Type 6:** Trust, Assurance, Stability
- **Type 5:** Clarity, Curiosity, Wonder

Heart Center: Love

- **Type 4:** Belonging, Beauty, Authenticity
- **Type 3:** Value, Worth, Wholeness
- **Type 2:** Compassion, Kindness, Nurturance

Gut Center: Power

- **Type 1:** Integrity, Perfection, Alignment
- **Type 9:** Harmony, Unity, Balance
- **Type 8:** Empowerment, Justice, Strength

PERSONALITY FIXATION

Are you wondering why the qualities of your essence seem abstract? They are, after all, your true nature...

The answer traces back to childhood development, which shifts our focus from our inherent inner essence to an externally focused and conditioned version of ourselves. This shift—from being naturally nourished by our inner essence to seeking fulfillment through external factors—leads to what the Enneagram community refers to as **fixation**.

Enneagram teachings on the origins of our personality fixations vary between nature and nurture, but the most common understanding is that while we are born with a predisposition for our primary type, our childhood conditioning shapes how this type fixates. Our upbringing,

ORIGINS, ESSENCE, & PERSONALITY

the challenges we face, and our cultural values all play critical roles in forming our predisposed personality fixations, as outlined by the Enneagram.

My goal is to demonstrate how the Enneagram acts as a guiding light, leading us back to the essence of our primary type and helping us reclaim the wholeness we were born to embody. This journey involves a deep exploration of our personality traits, starting with those of our primary type and extending to our connections with all the types.

TRAITS OF YOUR PERSONALITY

The Enneagram outlines nine distinct personality types, each with unique traits that developed as coping mechanisms to help you navigate stress and reconnect with the essential nourishment lost during early years. To clarify these traits, I've organized them into five specific categories.

Original Enneagram teachings, particularly those by Oscar Ichazo and Claudia Naranjo, include various categories like holy ideas and passions. I have carefully selected the following categories because I find them to be the most useful and practical. Over many years and decades, my focus has been on exploring aspects of the Enneagram that truly enrich our lives.

Over time, I have moved away from some labels and categories that reflect a different era in our understanding of the human condition, particularly the 60s and 70s, when Ichazo and Naranjo were pioneering the Enneagram.

Here are the categories I find most useful, which you will find repeated in each chapter for each type:

- **Nicknames:** I'll unpack the three main nicknames commonly used in the Enneagram community for each type.
- **Desire:** The core longing or motivation driving each type.

- **Emotion:** The primary emotion each type grapples with and how they process or cope with it.
- **Fixation:** The habitual focus or obsession for each type.
- **Shadow:** The unconscious aspects each type neglects or disowns.

Understanding these traits as survival tactics paves the way for personal growth. This reframing transforms the Enneagram from a mere classification system into a holistic guide for healing and growth.

Before we dive any further, it's important to grasp two foundational layers of the Enneagram—the three Centers and the three Energetic Directions. Even if you're familiar with the nine types, **don't overlook this next crucial part.**

THREE CENTERS & DIRECTIONS

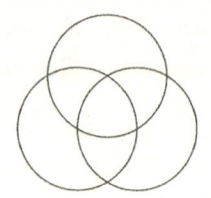

THREE CENTERS OF AWARENESS

At the core of the Enneagram lies the concept of three centers of awareness. These centers serve as a lens through which you experience and engage with life, each marked by a primary emotion and essence.

You navigate the world through these three centers: the head (your intellectual realm), the heart (your emotional domain), and the gut (your instinctual foundation).

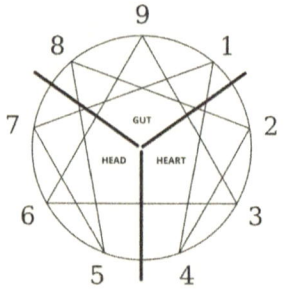

Head Center (Types 5, 6, 7)
Your Head Center resonates with the emotion of **fear**, yet it's the essence of **wisdom** that truly defines it. Within this space, you explore beliefs, visions, and intricate thought processes, always in pursuit of clarity and deeper understanding. Guided by analytical thought and

structured frameworks, you experience life by connecting the dots, discerning patterns, and gathering profound insights.

Key Elements—

- **Emotion:** Fear
- **Essence:** Wisdom
- **Perception:** Experiencing life through thought processes—analytical logic, reason, planning, beliefs, visions, structured thoughts and frameworks.
- **Seeks:** Clarity, understanding, security, and innovation.

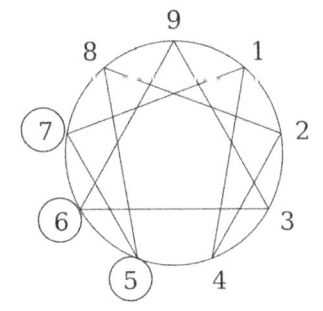

Ever find yourself immersed in contemplation, analyzing an idea? That's your head center doing its remarkable work.

Heart Center (Types 2, 3, 4)

Your Heart Center resonates with the emotion of **sadness**, yet it's the essence of **love** that truly defines it. In this realm, you navigate the world through your emotions, values, and relationships. You're on a quest for love, recognition, and a sense of worth—and the connections you form are guided by emotions and sentiments.

Key Elements—

- **Emotion:** Sadness
- **Essence:** Love
- **Perception:** Experiencing life through relationships, emotions, values, and interpersonal connections
- **Seeking:** Appreciation, value, emotional connection, and

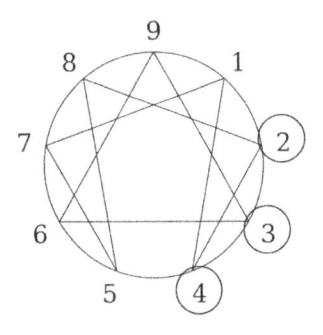

THREE CENTERS & DIRECTIONS

belonging.

You know those moments when your emotions really tug at your heartstrings—seeking love and value? That's your heart center at play.

Gut Center (Types 8, 9, 1)
Your Gut Center resonates with the emotion of **anger**, yet it's the essence of **power** that truly defines it. In this realm, you respond to life's twists and turns through instinct and gut reactions. Driven by a guttural intuition and a sense of right or wrong, you navigate the world through instinctive wisdom.

Key Elements—

- **Emotion:** Anger
- **Essence:** Power
- **Perception:** Experiencing life through impulses, intuition, instincts, biological reactions, and a guttural sense of right and wrong
- **Seeking:** Autonomy, influence, harmony, and integrity

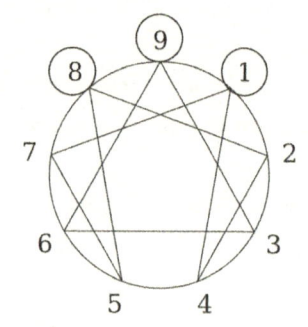

Ever had a 'gut feeling' about something? That instinct? That's your gut center in action.

While you lead with one specific center, you are still a blend of all three centers—head, heart, and gut.

Now that you're familiar with the backbone of the Enneagram, the three centers, let's explore the next layer of complexity that gives rise to the nine unique types—the three energetic directions.

THREE ENERGETIC DIRECTIONS

Beyond the foundation of the three centers, the Enneagram is further organized into three energetic directions. These directions repeat within each of your three centers (head, heart, and gut).

While, "energetic directions" is not a standardized term in the Enneagram literature, think of them as 'tuning knobs' that adjust how you experience and engage with yourself and the world. They influence whether you turn your focus inward, project it outward, or strive for a balanced approach.

To illustrate, consider the Heart center, associated primarily with love and sadness. Your dominant direction will shape how you experience your heart center. An outward focus (Type 2) means you express love and sadness externally, an inward focus (Type 4) leads you to internalize your emotion, and a balanced focus (Type 3) aims to harmonize your inner feelings with your external environment.

Why is this layer important?

It's at this level that the Enneagram evolves from a model focused on three basic centers to a nuanced framework of nine distinct types. This adds the depth and complexity that makes the Enneagram such a compelling and useful guide.

Let's dive into the details of each direction, exploring how they shape your attention, emotions, and identity within each center.

INWARD FACING—INTERNALIZING TYPES (5, 4, 1)

When you're primarily focused on your inner world, you are embodying the "inward" direction. This focus influences how you handle your primary emotions, leading you to internalize and suppress them. Here, your identity is shaped by your internal world. This inward potential is present in each of your three centers.

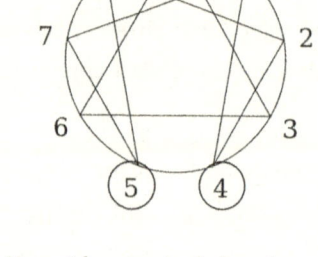

THREE CENTERS & DIRECTIONS

Have you ever felt deeply connected to your innermost thoughts, feelings, and instincts? That pull towards introspection? That's the inward direction in action.

- **Inward Head (Type 5):** Your attention is focused on the thoughts and ideas within your mind. You internalize or hold-in fear. Your identity is defined by your own ideas and mental activities.

- **Inward Heart (Type 4):** Your attention is focused on the emotions and moods within your heart. You internalize or hold-in sadness. Your identity is defined by your own emotions and desires.

- **Inward Gut (Type 1):** Your attention is focused on the instincts and drives within your body. You internalize or hold-in anger. Your identity is defined by your own impulses and behavioral responses.

BALANCED—NEUTRALIZING CORE TYPES (3, 6, 9)

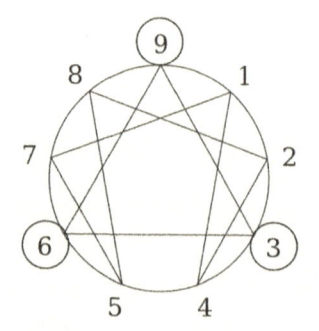

When you are balancing your focus between your internal and external worlds, you are embodying the "balanced" direction. This focus influences how you handle your primary emotions, leading you to balance and neutralize them. Here, your identity is shaped by this blend of inner and outer experiences. This balanced potential is present in each of your three centers.

THREE CENTERS & DIRECTIONS

Ever felt a tug to align your inner feelings, beliefs, and instincts with the world around you? That's the balanced direction at work.

- **Balanced Head (Type 6):** Your attention shifts between your own ideas and the views of those around you. You neutralize or avoid fear. Your identity is defined by aligning your views with those around you, either by adjusting your own ideas or seeking adjustments from others.

- **Balanced Heart (Type 3):** Your attention shifts between your own emotions and the feelings of those around you. You neutralize or avoid sadness. Your identity is defined by aligning your emotions with those around you, either by adjusting your own expression or seeking adjustments from others.

- **Balanced Gut (Type 9):** Your attention shifts between your own instincts and the behaviors of those around you. You neutralize or avoid anger. Your identity is defined by aligning your actions with those around you, either by adjusting your own behaviors or seeking adjustments from others.

OUTWARD FACING—EXTERNALIZING TYPES (2, 7, 8)

When you're primarily focused on your external world, you are embodying the "outward" direction. This focus influences how you handle your primary emotions, leading you to externalize and project them. Here, your identity is shaped by how you engage with the world around you. This outward potential is present in each of your three centers.

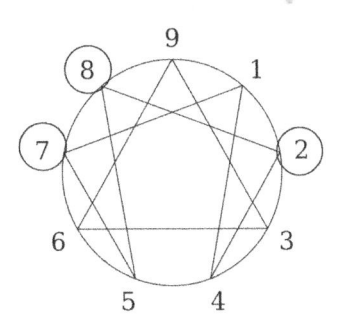

THREE CENTERS & DIRECTIONS

Ever found yourself drawn to the energy and dynamics of the world outside? That urge to engage? That's your outward direction shining through.

- **Outward Head (Type 7):** Your attention is focused on the ideas and knowledge that exist outside of you. You externalize or project fear. Your identity is defined by how you engage with the wisdom and ideals of the world around you.

- **Outward Heart (Type 2):** Your attention is focused on the emotions and moods of those around you. You externalize or project sadness. Your identity is defined by how you engage with the emotions and needs of those around you.

- **Outward Gut (Type 8):** Your attention is focused on the instincts and drives of those around you. You externalize or project anger. Your identity is defined by how you engage with the behaviors and impulses of those around you.

QUICK GUIDE TO THE ENERGETIC DIRECTIONS

Head Center: Wisdom, Fear, Intellect

- **Type 7:** Outward and Externalizing
- **Type 6:** Balanced and Neutralizing
- **Type 5:** Inward and Internalizing

Heart Center: Love, Sadness, Relational

- **Type 4:** Inward and Internalizing
- **Type 3:** Balanced and Neutralizing
- **Type 2:** Outward and Externalizing

Gut Center: Power, Anger, Instinctual

- **Type 1:** Inward and Internalizing
- **Type 9:** Balanced and Neutralizing
- **Type 8:** Outward and Externalizing

While you lead with a specific center and direction, defining your primary Enneagram type, you still encompass elements from all three centers and their three directions—including traits and qualities from all nine types.

WHOLENESS & EMBODIMENT

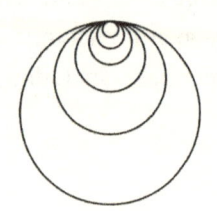

ARE YOU MORE THAN A TYPE?

I have personally witnessed hundreds of Enneagram journeys and one recurring theme has always stood out—everyone I've encountered resonates deeply with more than one type.

There are numerous theories that try to explain this. Some open the door to our multifaceted nature while others push us tighter into a singular type.

Then there's the hot issue of mistyping, which has carved its own unique space, attracting experts and tests dedicated to addressing it.

Yet, the simplest and most resonant explanation?

We embody all nine types, and the Enneagram is meant to illustrate our inherent wholeness. This simple yet pivotal insight dawned on me through my inner experience.

After studying the Enneagram for decades and deeply engaging with my primary type, I began to recognize how other types manifest in my personality traits, perceptions, and even core motivations. I observed this multifaceted reality in others as well—each client's story and every student's insight reflected the complex interplay of different types within their personalities.

During my certification program, as we explore each Enneagram type in depth, students consistently discover aspects of themselves in multiple types, often relating to all nine.

And why wouldn't they?

At its core, the Enneagram, with its three centers, asserts our multifaceted nature. Think about it, have you ever encountered someone lacking a head, heart, or gut?

In my recent Enneagram program, three students experienced a true resonance with every type we explored. With each new type, they felt they'd found their primary—only to reconsider as we delved into the next. It was a beautiful illustration of our multifaceted nature.

By the end of the program, each participant had identified their primary type: one aligned with Type 4, another with Type 7, and the third with Type 6. However, their understanding didn't stop there.

Using the Enneagram as a model for wholeness enabled them to go beyond merely identifying their primary type. Instead, they explored how aspects of each type manifest within them.

MISIDENTIFICATION OR WHOLENESS?

In the Enneagram community, there's a common belief that identifying with various types is just a characteristic of Types 6 and 9, rather than a true experience of our multifaceted nature. The notion that certain Enneagram types are more prone to "misidentifying" with multiple types is a misunderstanding. Certain types *may* more readily recognize multiple types within, but this reality is not exclusive to them.

WHOLENESS & EMBODIMENT

I invite you to pause and reflect on your own experience with any system that categorizes human nature.

What does it feel like to consider that you hold more than one type?

When I bring this up with people, their resonance and relief is often palpable—as though the wisdom of their direct experience has been validated.

To move *beyond* insight and really grow with the Enneagram, it's essential to embrace all the facets of your essence—each providing a distinct form of nourishment. Finding yourself in only one Enneagram type limits your opportunities for practical growth. The essence of each type acts as a universal nutrient, together forming a comprehensive resource for your whole self.

Imagine your psyche and its underlying essence as a tapestry, woven from nine distinct threads, each symbolizing a different Enneagram type. While some threads are denser, filling up more of the tapestry, all nine threads are present, contributing to its complete design.

Embracing your essence and wholeness is a tangible, physical journey. Let's delve into the science of embodiment to shed light on how somatic practices can turn insights of the Enneagram into a lived reality.

THE SCIENCE OF EMBODIMENT—A SOMATIC APPROACH TO THE ENNEAGRAM

In this book, I weave together the theories and practices of somatic psychology with the Enneagram, transforming it from a personality typing system into a tangible path for deep, comprehensive growth. This approach isn't just intuitive—it's rooted in the solid science of psychophysiology and somatic psychology.

Psychophysiology, a field supported by extensive research, explores the intricate connections between your mental, emotional, and physical states. Its findings validate the mind-body link, which is central to the essence practices in this book. These practices, driven by established scientific research, are grounded with empirical credibility.

Somatic psychology, a close ally of psychophysiology, focuses on healing and wellness through body awareness. It teaches us that our bodies hold onto stress and that engaging in specific somatic practices can facilitate healing and release.

THE ESSENCE EMBODIMENT PATH

The Enneagram of Essence introduces a fundamental path to engage with, cultivate, and embody the unique essence of each type.

Delving into the somatic realm, this path encourages the exploration of each type's core qualities through practical, sensory-based exercises. It combines somatic therapy techniques like 'Resourcing' to discover personal connections to essence, 'Grounding' to embody these qualities deeply within, and 'Pendulation' to navigate between the stress of personality patterns and the relief of connecting with essence. These practices aim to alleviate personality-driven stress while nurturing inner resources.

Simultaneously, this path addresses the need to consciously step away from habitual coping mechanisms identified in traditional Enneagram teachings as limiting traits. By identifying and gently reducing reliance on these traits, you create the necessary space to cultivate positive qualities and behaviors that align more closely with your true essence. This process not only detaches you from unhelpful habits but also enriches your life with practices that nourish and affirm your deepest self.

By actively engaging with this path, you embark on a journey to embody your type's essence more fully in everyday life, paving the way for a richer, more authentic existence.

LANGUAGE—INCLUSIVE AND SECULAR

In this book, I've chosen language that aims to bridge the gap often found in Enneagram literature. On one hand, many sources use religious and spiritual language, potentially alienating some readers. On the other hand, academic approaches often overlook essence, focusing too heavily on detailed personality patterns.

Essence transcends the theoretical boundaries of religion and science, connecting us all on a deeper level. This is a secular approach that celebrates both the Enneagram's mystical and psychological aspects, blending them for a holistic perspective.

READING GUIDE

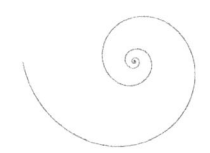

HOW TO READ THIS BOOK

I've crafted this book to be a step-by-step journey through your personal wholeness. I use second-person language to encourage you to delve into each type introspectively—regardless of whether it's your primary type.

In my training programs, where participants immerse into each type for a month, there's been a trend. Regardless of their primary type, most participants find it more familiar to begin with their head center and then progress downward—head to heart to gut.

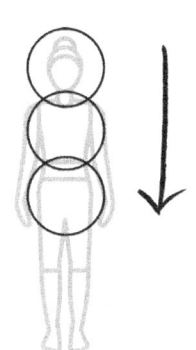

Therefore, this book is structured to be a personal journey from the top down—starting with Type 7 in your head center and flowing down through your being—around the Enneagram counterclockwise.

READING GUIDE

After exploring the joyful abundance of Type 7, you'll delve into the assuring trust of Type 6 and the insightful clarity of Type 5.

Then, descend into the landscape of your heart, uncovering the deep inner belonging of Type 4, the impressive dynamism of Type 3, and the nurturing warmth of Type 2.

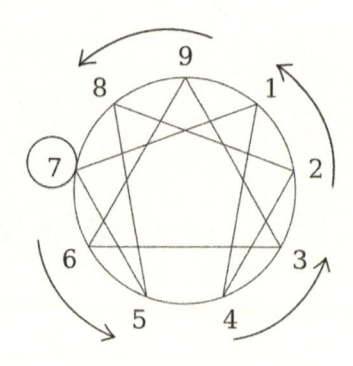

Finally, ground yourself in your gut center, culminating your journey with the pure integrity of Type 1, the balancing harmony of Type 9, and the empowered justice of Type 8.

That said, trust your intuition.

Feel free to explore the book in any order that resonates with you. This book intentionally repeats structures, titles, and guidance across every type to facilitate easy comparison and familiar navigation. The extensive use of titles and subtitles makes it easy to flip through and revisit specific sections as you wish.

Engage actively in this hands-on journey.

Within these pages, you'll discover practical exercises, relatable anecdotes, and guided meditations. Take your time, genuinely feel the essence of each type, and let the Enneagram of Essence be your compass.

We're almost ready to dive in. But first, let's chat about laying the groundwork for your essence practice.

CRAFTING YOUR ESSENCE PRACTICE

If you'd like this journey to be practical, lay a foundation for your essence practice. This will deepen your experience with each type,

READING GUIDE

fostering a tangible connection with each essence, yourself, and the world around you.

1. Dedicate Time Daily—Like any practice, consistency is key. Set aside a special time each day to engage with the exercises and reflections.

2. Curate Your Special Space—This is where you will do your practice. Choose a quiet corner of your home that feels inviting. It could be a cozy nook in your bedroom, a serene spot in your garden, or a quiet space in your living room. Within your chosen space, consider setting up a small altar—a table or shelf where you place items that resonate with the essence you're working with.

3. Engage Your Senses—I will encourage you to incorporate sensory elements for each type—like scent (essential oils or candles), taste (a specific tea or drink that relates to the essence), touch (stones or other tactile reminders), sight (symbols or colors associated with the essence), and sound (soothing music or natural sounds).

4. Keep a Journal—Document your reflections, insights, and experiences. This can be a space where you ponder the guiding questions and note any changes or developments in your relationship with the essence.

5. Stay Open, Curious, and Empowered—Approach this practice with an open heart and mind. Feel empowered to make it your own. Each day might bring a different experience, and that's perfect. The aim is to make your connection and understanding tangible.

6. Community and Sharing—Consider sharing your experiences with a trusted friend or within a community. Engaging with others can offer different perspectives and enrich your understanding.

Beyond exploring the primary traits, this book offers specific steps, materials, and ingredients to help you connect with each type's essence.

Keep in mind, these suggestions are meant to inspire.

READING GUIDE

Feel free to modify them and make them your own, aligning with your unique needs and preferences.

Now that we've laid the groundwork, let's dive into the nourishing world of the Enneagram of Essence. Turn the page with an open mind and get ready to embrace your Wisdom Center.

YOUR HEAD CENTER

SANCTUARY OF YOUR MIND

WISDOM & FEAR

Have you ever experienced your head...

- As the spacious "field" of your mind?
- As a silence around, yet beyond, your passing thoughts?
- As an empty awareness from which your thoughts and insights arise?

Take a moment to reflect.
Place your hands gently on your head.
Sense into this center of your being.

Ponder these questions, letting insights emerge naturally:

1. What kind of thoughts arise most often within your mind?
2. What do these thoughts feel like? Are they subtle or all-consuming?
3. How does your head space differ from these passing thoughts?
4. What sensations arise when you tap into the underlying awareness of your head center?

5. Are there specific moments when you really feel this quiet awareness?
6. What words describe this space—the *essence* of your head center?

Allow these questions to linger in your awareness, giving yourself the time and space to explore them fully.

HEAD CENTER ESSENCE — WISDOM

The essence of your Head Center is wisdom. This wisdom is not just a lofty concept—it is an awareness rooted in the inner stillness and quiet of your mind. Imagine the essence of your mind as a "fertile field", an abundant space where wonder, trust, and freedom emerge.

It's an awareness that seems to emanate from your head, serving as a silent canvas for your thoughts, questions, and ideas. A peaceful realm of wisdom beyond thought—true clarity, curiosity, assurance, and joy.

HEAD CENTER EMOTION — FEAR

Your Head Center is also the realm where you navigate the fog of fear and its relatives, worry and anxiety. Fear can feel like a dense fog that clouds your vision and grips your chest. It can make you feel isolated and paralyzed—churning your stomach and scrambling your thoughts.

However, when acknowledged and embraced, fear transforms into a compass—pointing you back to a nourishing experience of wisdom.

Think of fear as a fleeting cloud in the constant sky of your inner awareness. With attention and care, these clouds move on, leaving the expansive sky of your inherent wisdom. With practice, you can come to know this open sky is always there, holding space for your fears yet never defined by them.

I invite you to reconsider your relationship with fear. While it can feel like a tension, it's also a doorway to clarity and a connection to the spacious realm of your head center.

HEAD CENTER PERCEPTION — INTELLECTUAL

In your Head Center, you look at the world through an intellectual lens. This space serves as your mental workshop where you analyze, plan, and rationalize. It's the hub where you organize your abstract thoughts into concrete understandings that help you make sense of things. Here, your beliefs form, and your visions for the future crystallize. Logic and reason are your primary tools in this domain.

HEAD CENTER SEEKS — SECURITY

Your Head Center is more than just a thinking space, it's where you innovate and solve problems. It's your ground for intellectual pursuits —where life becomes a puzzle to solve, and where you engage in the quest for wisdom and understanding. You particularly enjoy using structured systems, like the Enneagram, to achieve these goals.

HEAD CENTER ENERGETIC DIRECTIONS

Type 7 (Outward): Your focus turns outwards—towards the world for engagement. Fear is transmuted into excitement and curiosity fuels adventure.

Type 6 (Balanced): Your focus is balanced—attuning your mind with the outer world. Fear is channeled into cautious discernment and curiosity is used to foster security and trust.

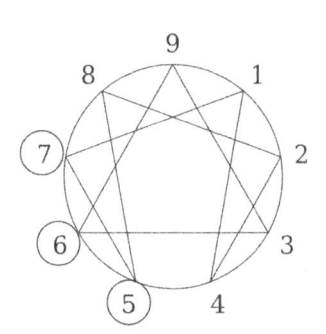

Type 5 (Inward): Your focus turns inward—into the mind for introspection. Fear is honed into insight and curiosity fuels deep understanding and clarity.

HEAD CENTER PRACTICES AND TRADITIONS

There are many cultural traditions and spiritual practices that emphasize the realm of the head, wisdom, and intellect. Here are just a few examples.

In spiritual contexts, Zen Buddhism emphasizes mindfulness meditation to discover the stillness of the mind. Similarly, the practice of studying ancient scriptures—like the Bhagavad Gita, the Bible, and the Tao Te Ching—nurtures cognitive realizations about the nature of life and our human essence.

New Age practices often include guided visualizations or affirmations aimed at reshaping thoughts and beliefs. These approaches focus on understanding, interpreting, and harnessing the power of the mind.

Examples:

- Mindfulness meditation
- Studying philosophical or religious texts
- Guided visualizations
- Affirmations
- Sound healing

With this foundation for the head center, let's conclude with a guided meditation. Immerse yourself in this portal into the essence of your head center, the sanctuary of your mind.

HEAD CENTER MEDITATION

I encourage you to find a comfortable position, relax your body, and gently soften your focus. Read this slowly and with ease, twice—first to visualize the imagery, and then again to deeply connect with the sensations it evokes.

Draw in a deep, nourishing breath.
Tune in to your head center.

Feel the sensation of your crown.
Feel your forehead and the back of your head.
Feel the space behind your eyes.

Notice any tension.
Gently invite it to relax.

Notice your thoughts passing through.
Movements of curiosity and clarity.

Imagine your mind as the spacious sky,
clear, open, and boundless.

Within this vastness,
thoughts flow through like clouds,
shaping your perceptions.

Each thought is distinct.
Each thought is temporary.

HEAD CENTER MEDITATION

*Behind these passing clouds,
is an ever-present,
spacious awareness.*

*Notice . . .
Most of the sky of your mind
is vast, empty, cloudless.*

*Peaceful, joyful, free.
Filled with wonder,
curiosity, and trust.*

*Feel its presence as a wise awareness,
a stillness that's always there,
ready to guide and nourish you.*

Pause for a moment.

How did that meditation feel? Did you experience the spacious "sky" of your mind?

If that meditation resonated, it's because you tapped into the sanctuary of your mind—the spaciousness beyond your passing thoughts. Remember, you do not need to silence your thoughts in order to experience the nourishment of your head center.

HEAD CENTER MEDITATION

With this general understanding, let's delve into the manifestations of your head center in its three types, beginning with the outward brilliance of Type 7, where joy and freedom dance hand in hand.

TYPE 7—FREEDOM

JOY & ABUNDANCE

KEY ELEMENTS

- **Center**—Head, Wisdom, and Fear
- **Direction**—Outward Focus
- **Personality**—Enthusiast Adventurer
- **Essence**—Joy, Freedom, Inner Abundance

Do you ever find yourself...

- Feeling an overflowing enthusiasm for the next adventure?
- Believing that more happiness is just one experience away?
- Feeling confined by daily routine and predictability?

There is a part of your personality that dances to the enthusiastic vibe of Type 7. And beyond these traits, your essence resonates with its joyful nourishment.

TYPE 7—FREEDOM

Have you ever felt...

- A quiet joy in life's simple, often overlooked moments?
- A freedom that transcends the thrill of new adventures?
- An abundance that embraces both joy and sorrow?

We've all got a hint of the Type 7 abundance within—a mind that craves exploration and joy. We all need a moment of novelty in a world that feels too mundane. The essence of this type is a doorway to an inner freedom that embraces the totality of human experience.

Consider this a call to stop chasing highs and avoiding lows.

Instead, cultivate a sense of freedom that can hold both the good times and the tough ones, the joys and the sorrows. By embracing this essence, you become an example of authentic joy in a world that overlooks the simple, playfulness of life. Let me tell you about the Type 7 part of me.

THAT PART OF ME THAT DREAMS OF GREENER GRASSES

> While Type 7 is not my core type, I've grown fond of its vibrant energy and wanderlust spirit within me. Whether Type 7 is a spark that occasionally ignites or the central fire of your being, I hope my story inspires you to find your own.
>
> In my life, Type 7 reveals itself as a quest for the novel and extraordinary, particularly when it comes to where I live. There's also this sensation of confinement, a restlessness, when my surroundings become too familiar.
>
> I've spent years seeking new towns and homes, in search of that perfect match to the ever-changing idyllic image in my mind.

TYPE 7—FREEDOM

My restless chase for the new, turning each place into a dream to be fulfilled, left a trail of broken leases and flipped houses. But beyond that, my Type 7 fixations pulled me farther away from the essence I truly needed.

Taking a moment to step back and really look inward was a game-changer for me. I realized that the sense of freedom I was chasing by staying on the move was actually within me all along. And let me tell you, this inner revelation feels more exhilarating than any new neighborhood or exotic location.

It was like stumbling upon a hidden treasure in my own backyard—realizing that I carried the keys to my own freedom within me, all the time.

I'll revisit this story at the end of the chapter and share how slowing down transformed my life and how I found a surprising joy in maintaining a routine. But first, let's unpack all the details of this type.

And as we move along, you might sense the echo of Type 7 within you, nudging you to embrace a playful nature and anchor yourself in the sources of true fulfillment.

Let's pause.
Breathe in the present moment.
And, get ready for a joyful ride.

WELCOME TO TRUE FREEDOM

The best way to begin is by tuning into the radiant essence of Type 7 already within you. Imagine a light sparkling behind your eyes—a bridge to a sense of joy that's always available, within your own presence.

It's like you have a spirited companion inside—who embodies the natural sense of delight the universe has to offer.

Picture a version of yourself where freedom isn't a fleeting sensation, but a foundational aspect of who you are. This level of joy doesn't come from chasing temporary highs—it isn't tied to conditions or circumstances. It's a steady glow that lights your path regardless of what comes your way.

Imagine you planned for a joyous Saturday hike, but your partner needs to talk about something serious. Instead of feeling like your freedom is compromised, you embrace this expression of life and find a rich contentment in being present and supportive. Your joy isn't tied to plans—it's a deeper part of who you are, ready to meet whatever comes your way.

Sounds like an invigorating journey, right?

You were born with an inherent sense of joy, shining naturally like a sunlit stream. But, as life's challenges unfolded, this luminous connection to your essence began to fade. In the face of stress, your Type 7 traits surfaced as survival mechanisms, distancing you from the abundant essence you were once immersed within.

This shift led you to develop a superficial optimism, propelling you on an endless quest for external pleasures.

This is where the Enneagram becomes invaluable. It acts as your personal lantern, lighting the path from superficial excitement to profound joy. It helps you understand that your personality fixations are symptoms of a deeper yearning to reconnect with your essence.

Let's delve into the fundamental relationship between the personality traits of Type 7 and its essence.

TYPE 7—FREEDOM

TYPE 7'S QUEST FOR JOY

Your Type 7 traits formed under stress, pulling your focus away from inner essence, and prompting you to pursue joy externally. You've been seeking freedom and fulfillment by creating adventure and novelty.

This external search keeps your attention on the move, overlooking the true abundance present in ordinary, everyday life. Consider my Type 7 experience of chasing new living environments. This constant moving made me miss the contentment found by anchoring my life in the present.

To relax my Type 7 fixations, I had to pause my on-going pursuit of new and different living environments. Focusing instead on finding my sense of novelty and abundance within, which brought a more enduring sense of satisfaction.

Have there been moments when your search for a new, more exciting experience blinded you from joy in the here and now?

Here's a piece of Enneagram wisdom—every trait of the Enthusiastic Explorer is an imitation of its essence. Your passion for adventure? It echoes the essence of universal freedom. The continual craving for novelty? It's your personality's way of mimicking the essence of universal abundance.

Remember that the traits we're about to explore stem from a deeper longing for authentic joy, freedom, and abundance. Each one offers a chance to connect more deeply with your inner essence.

Take a moment to ponder these questions:

1. Do you ever plan for something better to avoid the present? What drives this?
2. Do you ever chaser new experiences? What are you really looking for?
3. Ever feel trapped? What activates this feeling?

TYPE 7—FREEDOM

4. How do you react when feeling confined?
5. Can you find freedom within daily responsibilities?
6. When did you last experience true joy? Was it sparked by something outside or within you?

Allow these questions linger and return to them for deeper contemplation. Now let's journey back to childhood and uncover the origins of your Type 7 traits.

CHILDHOOD OF TYPE 7 — ESSENCE TO FIXATION

Reflect on your childhood through the Type 7 lens. Memories of a vibrant, always-curious youngster might surface—always on the hunt for the next adventure.

The world was your playground and you reveled in its endless wonders. Each day brought a new mission—charting the backyard's tiniest mysteries or gazing up, lost in the patterns of the skies. You'd jump from one hobby to another, from collecting cards to learning the guitar, because why not? You never wanted to miss out on anything.

Yet amid all this wonder, an emptiness lingered.

A yearning for more affection quietly carved out those Type 7 tendencies—urging you to seek novelty to fill that void. Remember the fidgety feeling when a class dragged on or routine tasks seemed never-ending? That itch for more brewed into low-level anxiety when life's pace wasn't on par with your zest.

But through it all, your bright spirit was a magnet. Your pure delight in life's simplest joys not only uplifted your spirits but also those around you. It wasn't just about finding joy for yourself—it was about sharing it. Today, your optimism, curiosity, and sense of adventure trace back to that wonder-filled child.

With these memories as our foundation, let's unpack the personality traits of Type 7, as reflected in its most popular nicknames.

TYPE 7—FREEDOM

TYPE 7 NICKNAMES

The Epicure

Your refined taste and appreciation for quality, earned you this nickname. You have a knack for elevating even the most delightful moments with an extra dose of magic. Whether it's adjusting the ambiance to the perfect lighting, selecting touching music, or presenting a special treat that brings joy, your ability to craft unforgettable experiences is exceptional. You are always fine-tuning your surroundings to achieve a peak of enjoyment and aesthetic pleasure.

Your quest for the finest transcends traditional pleasures, exploring the depths of various subcultures and interests with unwavering enthusiasm. Whether it's the art of mushroom foraging, the rich aromas of single-origin coffees, or the purity of the finest drinking water, you are equally enthralled. Your discerning taste knows no bounds, always in search of unparalleled quality in the most unexpected places.

While you're skilled at crafting delightful moments, remember, your high standards often create the negativity you wish to avoid. Your idealistic expectations can backfire, leading to disappointment when reality doesn't match your perfect vision.

The Wanderlust

This nickname captures your desire for exploration and new experiences. For you, staying in one place for too long feels restrictive—you're driven to immerse yourself in diverse cultures, relish the unfamiliar, and embrace the joys of new mysteries.

You embody the free-spirited wanderer—prioritizing dynamic experiences and always keeping the doors open for the next adventure.

However, this perpetual quest for excitement leads to challenges in decision-making and commitment, as the allure of more enriching experiences always beckons.

The Enthusiast

Radiating with exuberance, you bring life and color wherever you go. Your magnetic energy and passion are undeniable, captivating others into your world of excitement and joy. People can't help but be uplifted by your genuine optimism and spirited approach to the present.

Yet, beneath this fun-loving exterior, there's a subtler dynamic at play—your enthusiasm is often an unconscious stress response rather than a true reflection of your essence. Your authentic nature is characterized more by serene bliss than by enthusiastic exuberance.

MEET ALEX, AN ENTHUSIASTIC NEW AGE SEEKER

> Step into the world of my friend Alex, an exuberant Type 7 with a New Age flair. He's known for his boundless enthusiasm and quest for life's higher meanings. He has a lovely way of weaving spiritual ideas into his everyday conversations—but he also uses them as a shield against negativity.
>
> Alex's relationship with his partner, Mark, a soulful Type 4, paints a vivid picture of this dynamic.
>
> When confronted with serious or uncomfortable discussions, Alex retreats into his metaphysical sanctuary. With remarks like "The universe has a plan" or "We're the architects of our experiences," he deflects any perceived negativity and cloaks himself in a layer of New Age ideals.
>
> This doesn't sit well with Mark, whose Type 4 essence craves emotional authenticity. Mark feels overshadowed and unheard

TYPE 7—FREEDOM

amidst Alex's enthusiastic detours. Alex's spiritual jargon, while well intentioned, is a barrier to deeper emotional intimacy.

The Enneagram is helping Alex recognize his strong Type 7 nature and discover that holistic growth involves more than chasing joy and excitement—it also means facing his shadows. He's realizing that embracing the full spectrum of life, its highs and lows, is essential. True joy, after all, is abundant enough to embrace both radiance and darkness.

Each of these nicknames holds a tapestry of many threads—let's explore these characteristics with the spirited curiosity of Type 7.

PERSONALITY TRAITS OF TYPE 7

Desire: All Pleasure, No Pain

Your core longing is for a life steeped in unending pleasure and devoid of discomfort. Deep down, you desire to glide effortlessly from one blissful moment to the next, in perpetual happiness and freedom from life's harsh realities. This passion manifests as an insatiable appetite for joyous experiences, a constant quest for novelty, and an aversion to anything that hints at suffering.

You often skim the surface, hopping from thrill to thrill, inadvertently missing the rich spectrum of emotions and experiences that define a full life. True joy isn't about constant pleasure or avoiding pain—it's about embracing all of life's experiences. Recognizing this leads to a deeper, more meaningful happiness—one that integrates both joy and sorrow, pleasure and pain, offering a balanced and authentic life experience.

TYPE 7—FREEDOM

Emotion: Restless Enthusiasm (Externalized Fear)

As the outward-orienting head type, you externalize the fear that governs the head center—transmuting it into restless enthusiasm. You use peak experiences to divert your attention away from fear and prevent it from bringing you down. This may lead you to believe you're always satisfied, but this gluttony reflects an underlying restlessness.

Indeed, despite your efforts to escape it, fear shapes your choices and actions.

You have a deep-rooted fear of being trapped, which propels you to plan, move from one experience to the next, and keep your options open. Recognizing this tendency to run away or escape is essential for your personal growth and self-awareness. By staying present and feeling your fear, you will develop resilience and find satisfaction that sustains itself naturally.

Fixation: Anticipation of Pleasant Experiences

To some extent you are always planning and dreaming about future adventures, experiences, and opportunities. It's like you have a mental calendar, constantly filled with the promise of something better coming up—be it a weekend getaway, a concert, or a new project at work.

This forward-looking mindset serves as your personal buffer against feelings of boredom, confinement, and pain.

For example, imagine being stuck in a traffic jam. Instead of focusing on the annoyance of the moment, you find yourself excitedly planning your next vacation, contemplating all the sights you'll see and the experiences you'll have. This anticipatory outlook reassures you that there's always something positive around the corner, making the present moment more bearable.

TYPE 7—FREEDOM

Shadow: Insatiability and Inner Poverty

Beneath your vibrant surface lies a shadow of insatiability, rooted in an internal sense of lack and inner poverty—stemming back to childhood. This shadow drives your unending search for more, blocking your ability to fully appreciate the abundance and freedom already present in your life.

Facing this insatiable appetite is essential to finding true fulfillment. Recognize this deep-seated yearning and nurture it with an internal sense of abundance. As you cultivate fulfillment from within, you'll find a richer appreciation for life's current circumstances, overcoming the need for perpetual external pleasures.

MEET EMMA, WITH A PASSION FOR WELLNESS RETREATS

> My delightful client, Emma, a vivacious Type 7, has an insatiable thirst for self-help exploration. Although she seems invigorated by each retreat she attends, her pursuits are driven by a quest for something more, something even deeper.
>
> For Emma, the joy from these retreats is fleeting. She constantly scans the horizon for another, hoping the next will offer an even more transformative experience. The mere act of selecting one leaves her anxious, haunted by the "what ifs" of missing a potentially life-altering experience.
>
> However, Emma's self-awareness has blossomed. She's learning to anchor herself in the essence of her Type 7, realizing that true fulfillment can be nurtured from within. As she progresses on this introspective journey, she's becoming more discerning, opting for fewer retreats and trusting her choices more.
>
> Through this transformative process, Emma has unearthed a

TYPE 7—FREEDOM

revelation—her Type 7 essence is a much deeper wellspring of nourishment than her wellness retreats. By balancing her external pursuits with an internal abundance, she's beginning to find the profound contentment she once sought in retreats.

Emma's journey beautifully illustrates the Type 7 spirit that resides within us all. But what does this type actually feel like from within? Let's dive into the sensations and experiences of Type 7 in your body, exploring the intricacies of both its personality and essence.

SOMATIC EXPERIENCE OF TYPE 7

Energetic Direction: Outward

Compared to the other head types—the Type 5 that turns inward or the Type 6 that balances—your Type 7 turns outward into the world, radiating your vibrant energy for all to feel. You seek to immerse in and influence the external environment, ensuring it reflects your inherent joy and enthusiasm.

For example, if you love last-minute adventures but your friend likes having a set itinerary, your Type 7 outward flowing enthusiasm might kick in, tempting you to persuade them to go with your flow.

In Stress: Enthusiastic

Beneath your skin, there's a buzzing energy—a zest for life that draws you toward every new experience. Your eyes dart around, hungry for the next adventure. Your step has a youthful bounce—a reflection of your insatiable curiosity.

Deep in your belly, there's a tension. It's the weight of always wanting more and the hidden anxieties you are trying to outrun. There's also a secret yearning lingering in your heart—an unmet need from

TYPE 7—FREEDOM

childhood that you've been attempting to satisfy through external thrills.

With Essence: Embodied Joy

As the restlessness of survival mode fades, true joy deepens into your being. Throughout your body, you feel an expansive freedom, like a bird soaring in open skies. Your breath is deep, rich with gratitude for life's simple beauties.

A warm joy rises from your core, lighting up your eyes with radiant wisdom. This joy animates your every gesture, adding a playful twinkle. And even in life's darkest times, your inner freedom stands open, ready to embrace highs *and* lows.

With this experience vivid in you, let's move to the last section and get to know the mature, truly free Type 7.

MATURE TYPE 7 — FIXATION TO ESSENCE

Fostering growth and maturity in your Type 7 revolves around embracing inner freedom—within yourself, in all your experiences, and in the fabric of life itself.

Picture yourself as a bird—once you flew restlessly in search of more, now you find beauty and contentment both in soaring the sky and in the stillness of your own nest.

Remember that insatiable desire for what's next?

Instead of always seeking another adventure, you find joy in the present. The future is no longer about the frantic search for something "better." Now, you revel in the present moment, enriched by an internal sense of abundance.

Your relentless quest for freedom has turned into something even better—a grounded sense of wisdom. It's like growing from being a free-spirited traveler who's always hopping from one place to the next,

TYPE 7—FREEDOM

into a wise journeyer who knows the value of staying put long enough to really understand and appreciate life.

This wisdom doesn't mean you've given up on adventure—rather, you've learned how to find meaning in both the exciting and the everyday.

You haven't lost your enthusiasm, it has deepened into something more sustainable and fulfilling. Instead of using your zest for life to escape discomfort, you've learned how to find a deep, calm happiness that not only enriches you but those around you. Your joy is anchored and spreads easily to those you interact with.

It's your balanced approach—embracing inner contentment as you savor life's rich tapestry—that makes you truly free.

Isn't it a remarkable journey?

With that, I'm excited to conclude this chapter by diving deeper into my own Type 7 experience. The highs and lows, the restless moments, and the growing wisdom that guides me towards true contentment.

TO BE FAIR, I HAVE ALWAYS DREAMT OF FAR-OFF LANDS

> From a young age, my heart danced with dreams of far-off lands. The enchantment of foreign cultures, the touch of time-worn temples, and the exotic flavors from different corners of the world drew me in.
>
> As I grew, these dreams evolved, centering around the perfect dwelling—from tranquil country homes to bustling city apartments, from lush jungles to serene beaches.
>
> This Type 7 longing has always nudged me towards the magical and novel.
>
> For me, home was never just bricks and mortar—it was where

my dreams took form. Every unfamiliar locale set my heart aflutter. I'd lose myself in daydreams, convincing myself, and my patient husband, that we'd found paradise.

But as the glow of novelty faded, reality would chip away at my rose-tinted visions. Broken leases, flipped houses, and the emotional toll of uprooting our family made it evident, I was caught in a Type 7 whirlwind—seeking external joy while overlooking the treasures within.

I began to introspect. My true quest wasn't about the perfect abode or thrilling adventures—it was a deeper, inner fulfillment I was after. True to the Type 7 essence, I began to understand that real abundance and freedom lie beyond life's temporary forms.

So, I made a conscious choice to abstain from my Type 7 impulses and ground my wanderlust.

We planted our roots into a homestead, teeming with projects for my extra energy. The joy of nurturing a constant, the serenity in stillness, and the satisfaction of seeing my work bear fruit in my backyard has been a revelation.

The physical reflection of this inner fulfillment isn't lost on me. Our home feels like a sanctuary, brimming with a deeper kind of abundance.

To my surprise, the simple act of observing the rhythm of the seasons from a familiar vantage point offers a freedom like none I've known before.

Thank you for accompanying me on this invigorating journey. I hope my stories and insights have ignited deeper introspection within you.

TYPE 7—FREEDOM

Next, you'll find practical steps for embodying your Type 7 essence, designed to help you move beyond limiting personality traits and integrate this wisdom into your daily life. These resources are an introduction to the embodiment path — setting the stage for deeper explorations available in my full programs.

For a FREE printable copy of this embodiment guide for all 9 types, please visit my website: EnneagramofEssence.com

TYPE 7—FREEDOM

EMBODIMENT
PATH TO FREEDOM
EMBRACING TYPE 7 ESSENCE

JOURNEY INTO ESSENCE
The Enneagram of Essence's practical power is rooted in embodying essence and releasing limiting patterns. This brief guide to embodying Type 7's freedom is my gift, setting the stage for a much deeper exploration available in my full programs.

JOY THROUGH TYPE 7 ESSENCE
Even though Type 7 is not my primary type, its essence brings freshness to my life, infusing me with playful energy—like the enthusiasm of a child. *How could Type 7 essence enrich your inner and outer world?*

NATURE'S FREEDOM
Consider the rush you feel when you're moments away from feeling the ocean waves tickle your feet, or the eager anticipation as the first snowflakes begin to dance in the sky. That's the effervescent spirit of Type 7.

MIND-BODY WELLNESS
Studies show embracing such childlike curiosity can alter physiological markers, easing your stress responses and brightening your outlook.

TYPE 7—FREEDOM

EMBODIMENT
PATH TO FREEDOM
EMBRACING TYPE 7 ESSENCE

STEP 1: IDENTIFY PORTALS TO JOY

Identify what ignites feelings of joy and freedom for you — nature, memories, bright people, etc. For me, watching a bird soar through the sky fills me with a sense of exhilarating freedom.

What symbols or experiences spark joy for you?

Incorporate elements like colors, textures, flavors, scents and sounds that mirror this quality into your space, as reminders of your Type 7 journey.

STEP 2: FEEL AND ANCHOR FREEDOM

Notice the distinct way freedom and joy feel within you. When I tap into this essence, I feel expansive, like a bird spreading it's wings and soaring — like the inner smile of the universe.

What does freedom feel like in your body?

Practice feeling and anchoring this essence deeply throughout your nervous system — visualize and feel it flow through you, influencing your posture, movements, and perceptions.

TYPE 7—FREEDOM

EMBODIMENT
PATH TO FREEDOM
EMBRACING TYPE 7 ESSENCE

STEP 3: CENTER FREEDOM

Make an effort to notice and value the essence of freedom, joy and abundance in people around you. Focus on essence when noticing someone's personality.

Think about how centering essence could change your understanding and appreciation of people with the primary Type 7.

How could this practice deepen your understanding and connections with people primarily identified as Type 7?

STEP 4: CREATE A PRACTICE

Incorporate these steps into a flexible and creative practice, bringing it into your daily routine from a week to a month. Focus on portals that ignite freedom and joy. Through regular engagement, embodying true abundance will become more and more effortless.

How will integrating these practices transform your daily life?

EMBODIMENT
PATH TO FREEDOM
EMBRACING TYPE 7 ESSENCE

STEP 5: ABSTAIN FROM LIMITING TRAITS

Make space within yourself to cultivate freedom. Type 7 personality traits serve as survival mechanisms so it's important to release them gently, leaning on inner resources for support.

Mindfully identify and release Type 7 patterns that detract from your essence, including:

RELENTLESS SEARCH FOR ADVENTURE
Find joy in the *simplicity* of life. Reflect on moments of genuine *inner* freedom.

OVERCOMMITMENT
Choose how you spend your time, be fully present in each moment, release other options.

AVOIDANCE OF DISCOMFORT
Embrace challenging emotions as opportunities for growth.

FOMO (FEAR OF MISSING OUT)
Anchor yourself in the present with reminders of inner joy, like the warmth of sunlight.

SURFACE OPTIMISM
Embrace a fuller spectrum of emotions for a more enriching life experience.

TYPE 7—FREEDOM

> **EMBODIMENT**
> # Path to Freedom
> **EMBRACING TYPE 7 ESSENCE**

STEP 5: ABSTAIN FROM LIMITING TRAITS

Mindfully identify and release Type 7 patterns that detract from your essence, including:

IMMEDIATE GRATIFICATION
Practice patience and mindfulness — anchor the sensation of inner freedom along your journey.

DISTRACTIBILITY
Focus more deeply, use sensory reminders to stay present and embrace the moment.

QUICK IMPULSIVITY
Pause to reflect on choices — make decisions from a place of inner joy and abundance.

SEEKING EXTERNAL STIMULATION
Find freedom in quietude, carry symbols that remind you of the joy in stillness.

OVER-ENTHUSIASM
Allow space for diverse emotions and remember life's varied experiences offer depth.

DREAD OF CONFINEMENT
View commitments as paths to abundance — use essence practices to navigate feelings of entrapment.

Embodiment
Path to Freedom
Embracing Type 7 Essence

Step 5: Abstain from Limiting Traits
Mindfully identify and release Type 7 patterns that detract from your essence, including:

Endless Activity
Value stillness, setting aside times for quiet reflection and practices that foster calm.

Jumping from One Thing to the Next
Engage deeply with each activity, exploring practices that encourage slowing down.

Over-Reliance on External Validation
Cultivate affirmation within, use personal symbols to remember your inner abundance.

Use Step 5 as a bridge, not fixed rules. By centering essence, your personality traits will naturally relax into the nourishing qualities of joy and freedom.

Let's conclude with a moment of integration through this guided meditation—opening the door to inner joy.

TYPE 7—FREEDOM

GUIDED MEDITATION FOR TYPE 7

I encourage you to find a comfortable position, relax your body, and gently soften your focus. Read this slowly and with ease, twice—first to visualize the imagery, and then again to deeply connect with the sensations it evokes.

Relax your shoulders.
Bring awareness into your body.

You're on a path.
Sandy and warm.
The ocean whispers ahead.
Inviting you.

Balmy air embraces.
Soothing your skin.

Breathe in.
Savor the scent.
Salty air, fresh and alive.

The sand,
soft beneath your feet.
Yielding.

Look...
Seagulls fly above.
Champions of joy.

© 2023 Enneagram of Essence. All rights reserved.

TYPE 7—FREEDOM

GUIDED MEDITATION FOR TYPE 7

Palm trees sway.
In rhythm with the ocean breeze.

Listen...
Waves gently murmur.
Calling.

Step by step.
You draw closer
to a warm adventure.

Sunlight streams
from high above.

Light reflects on the path,
hinting at hidden wonders.

As you draw closer,
the rhythm of the ocean
reverberates within.

Soft waves
meet you at the shore.
A serene hello.

Feel the cool water, toes first.
Mist on your face.
Refreshing. Invigorating.

© 2023 Enneagram of Essence. All rights reserved.

TYPE 7—FREEDOM

GUIDED MEDITATION FOR TYPE 7

Let the water rush past you.
A kiss of pure abundance.

You're not just on the beach.
With every wave
you remember
Inner joy and freedom.

Pause for a moment.

How did that meditation feel? Did you experience the serene joy of the ocean's embrace?

If that meditation resonated, it's because you accessed the spirit of joy, a quality that transcends external life. The ocean serves as a gateway, but remember, the essence of Type 7—joy and freedom—is inherently within you.

This is your journey. Absorb these suggestions at your pace—let them take root. Once Type 7 is grounded within you, turn the page and join me in unpacking the Type 6. Let's embrace your facets of universal trust and assurance.

© 2023 Enneagram of Essence. All rights reserved.

TYPE 6—TRUST

ASSURANCE & STABILITY

KEY ELEMENTS

- **Center**—Head, Wisdom, and Fear
- **Direction**—Balanced Focus
- **Personality**—Loyal Skeptic
- **Essence**—Trust, Assurance, Inner Stability

Do you ever find yourself...

- Looking for reasons not to trust people?
- Doubting your decisions, needing absolute certainty?
- Planning to ensure safety, looking for potential threats?
- Prioritizing loyalty to others over your own needs?

There is a part of your personality that has the skeptical vigilance of Type 6. And even deeper, your inner essence is attuned to its trusting nourishment.

TYPE 6—TRUST

Have you ever felt...

- Deep inner trust despite facing your worst fears?
- A solid sense of inner guidance in uncertain times?
- Clear, confident action when you needed it most?
- Like a pillar of support and loyalty in your community?

We all have a facet of Type 6 within—a mind that seeks security and assurance. We all want to know who and what to trust in an unpredictable world. The essence of this type is a gateway to an inner trust that can weather all of life's unpredictable storms.

Consider this a call to stop chasing safety through vigilance and questioning.

Instead, cultivate an internal assurance that can hold uncertainty. By embracing this essence, you become an example of stability, trust, and assurance in a world teeming with doubt and insecurity. Let me share about the part of me that resonates with Type 6.

THE PART OF ME THAT DREADS THE UNKNOWN

The Type 6 resonates deeply within me—it's my dominant type. Whether you identify strongly with Type 6, or find just a tinge of skepticism within, I hope my story inspires you to find your own.

In my twenties, my quest for well-being, clarity and peace became my main focus. Fueled by debilitating anxiety that stifled my dreams and dimmed my potential, I explored everything from psychotherapy to Eastern philosophies and New Age traditions.

The Enneagram became my compass and I directed all my efforts toward understanding my dominant Type 6.

TYPE 6—TRUST

My anxiety was a paralyzing fear of the unknown, manifesting in small but consuming ways. Whether agonizing over which major to choose in college or dreading social gatherings, the fear was ever-present. I'd spend restless nights envisioning all the ways I might feel out of place the next day—wondering, "Will I say the wrong thing, say too much, or not say enough?"

I was trapped in a Type 6 cycle.

Yet, after years of introspection, I began to experience relief from anxiety. I thought I had unearthed every hidden fear and shadowy corner associated with my Type 6 tendencies. Convinced I had done all the inner work needed for a peaceful life, I missed the heart of the matter—I was treating the symptoms, but not getting to the root cause.

As I stepped into my thirties, an unexpected chill shook my foundation—a discovery that made me question everything. It turns out, there were deeper layers of my garden to be nurtured—uncharted terrain that would lead me on a journey more profound than I had ever expected.

At the end of this chapter I'll share how embracing life's deepest uncertainties—and gazing into the depths of mortality—led me to discover the essence of the Enneagram.

As we go deeper into Type 6, I hope you begin to hear its essence within you, whispering reassurances, inspiring you to face deeper truths and ground yourself in what truly matters.

Take a pause.
Find your breath.
Prepare for a reassuring journey.

TYPE 6—TRUST

WELCOME TO TRUE TRUST

To start, let's find the essence of Type 6 within you. Imagine a solid sense of trust within you, as stable and enduring as an oak tree in a mature forest. It reflects in your eyes while grounding your entire being, resonating in your heart, gut, and anchoring down through your feet.

It's like having a trustworthy companion inside—guiding you to feel the stability and safety the universe can offer.

This trust is more than just a concept—it is a real, palpable feeling that comes from deep within you. And it's not just about trusting people, it's a fundamental sense of security and assurance in the universe and life itself.

Imagine presenting at a community meeting, typically a nerve-wracking scenario. As you walk to the front of the room, instead of obsessing over every possible scenario or question from the audience, an unexpected stability envelops you. It's not just confidence in your words, but a deeper, innate trust within yourself. This internal assurance makes you feel secure and at home, even in potentially risky situations.

It's quite a soothing part of yourself, don't you think?

You were born with a natural trust in life, as fluid and free as a river following its course. Yet, the challenges of childhood shook that reassuring essence. Your Type 6 traits kicked into survival mode, making you doubt and question.

This led you to become overly cautious and loyal, always on the lookout for something or someone trustworthy—desperately trying to reconnect with true assurance.

This is where the Enneagram becomes your personal guide—leading you away from reactive fears and back to a foundational state of inner trust. It helps you understand that your personality fixations are symptoms of a deeper yearning to reconnect with your essence.

Let's explore the fundamental relationship between the personality traits of Type 6 and its essence.

TYPE 6'S QUEST FOR ASSURANCE

Your Type 6 personality traits developed in response to past stress and trauma, pulling your focus away from essence and into a state of vigilant safety-seeking. You learned to look for trust in outside sources and got trapped in overthinking.

This vigilant seeking not only keeps you in a state of heightened anxiety but also limits your connections with others.

For example, as a mother I frequently find myself overwhelmed by worry for my children. This worry, while rooted in love, eats up moments that could be spent in pure presence with them. When I actively embrace my Type 6 essence, I channel trust and courage. This helps me focus on being with my children, letting my genuine love for them guide the way instead of being overshadowed by anxiety.

How do your worries overshadow precious moments with your loved ones? How could anchoring true trust change that experience?

Ponder this—every trait of the Loyal Skeptic is connected to its essence, universal trust. That over-the-top loyalty is a mere reflection of the genuine stability in universal trust. The skepticism, a quest for a reliable and secure environment, mirrors a deeper longing for trust in the universal order and its inherent stability.

As we delve deeper, approach each trait with this in mind, explore how each can be viewed as both an imitation and a subconscious pursuit of inner trust.

TYPE 6—TRUST

Take a moment to ponder these questions:

1. Do you ever crave safety and assurance? When and why?
2. Are you loyal? What or who do you feel most loyal to?
3. Does fear or anxiety guide your decisions?
4. Do you find yourself being skeptical or challenging leadership? Why?
5. How do you cope with doubt or indecision? What brings you trust?
6. When did you last feel true trust? Was it sparked by something outside or within you?

Let these questions linger with you and return to them for deeper reflection. Now let's explore how these Type 6 traits originated in your early years.

CHILDHOOD OF TYPE 6 — ESSENCE TO FIXATION

Looking back at your childhood through the lens of Type 6, waves of unpredictability might flood your memories.

Do you recall days tinted with insecurity? The palpable tension of not knowing what to expect next? Whether it was at home, school, or in your neighborhood, each setting posed its own set of uncertainties. You were the child always double-checking.

Did you frequently seek reassurance, asking adults those "what-if" questions or repeatedly confirming plans with friends, just to make sure they still stood?

And what about those guardians and mentors, who should've been your pillars? Sometimes, they felt more like stormy clouds than shelters. Their inconsistency, or perhaps their overprotection, felt unsettling or even threatening.

TYPE 6—TRUST

In navigating these stormy waters, you honed the skills of vigilance and anticipation. You became adept at predicting and preparing for problems before they could surprise you.

But here's something interesting. That uncertainty didn't push you away. Instead, you clung to the relationships and institutions that offered any sense of stability—forming incredibly loyal bonds.

That's what makes you such a committed friend and partner today.

Your strong sense of loyalty is more about dealing with life's uncertainties than showing your true self. It's like a safety net you've created because the world felt insecure.

With these memories as our backdrop, let's explore the personality traits of Type 6 through its most common nicknames.

TYPE 6 NICKNAMES

The Skeptic

Feeling vulnerable and unprotected in your early years led you to develop a keen sense of hyper-vigilance, always scanning for potential threats. This ingrained caution prompts you to question everything, particularly authority figures and institutional systems. At times, you misinterpret others' intentions through your skeptical lens.

Make no mistake, you doubt yourself as well. This inner uncertainty drives you to seek external reassurance and to gather as much information as possible in an endless pursuit of something truly reliable. By regularly testing the trustworthiness of the world around you, you're navigating life's unpredictability the only way you know how.

The Loyalist

TYPE 6—TRUST

For the Type 6 in you, loyalty isn't just a trait—it's a cornerstone of how you interact with the world. Your loyal tendencies stem from a profound need for trustworthy connections. In your search for security, you find solace in aligning yourself with reliable people, groups, and systems. Your unwavering support for those you trust makes you a dependable companion. By fostering a stable environment, you bring a sense of predictability not only to your own life but also to the lives of those around you.

The Guardian

Think of your guardian aspect as your personal security system. Whereas your loyal side focuses on building trustworthy relationships, your guardian side takes a step further by actively maintaining that trust through vigilance and protection. Protecting those you trust is both an expression of your affection and your way of ensuring they remain a part of your security system.

You are not just loyal—you're a natural protector who is always on the lookout for potential risks. Your guardian instincts work to maintain a safe and stable environment for yourself, your loved ones, and community. Using your keen eye and sharp mind, you're committed to keeping things secure and stable.

The Counter-Phobic

These three nicknames capture most of the primary traits of your Type 6, yet there's more depth to this personality. Type 6 has a unique spectrum—from phobic to counter-phobic. Phobic tendencies involve avoiding fears while counter-phobic tendencies mean confronting or seeking them out. Both are ways to cope with anxiety.

You possess both phobic and counter-phobic tendencies but gravitate more towards one. Most descriptions of Type 6 center on the phobic traits. Therefore, I dedicated a section to delve into the counter-phobic outliers that make this type so intriguing.

Your counter-phobic side tackles fear directly, replacing anxiety with a semblance of "courage". This part of you actively seeks challenges and embraces risks to master your insecurities.

Your independence, determination, and pseudo-bravery are inspiring. Yet, it's essential to understand that this counter-phobic demeanor *mimics* courage and stems from the same stress as your phobic tendencies. True courage emerges when you realign with your essence.

THAT TIME I DISCOVERED MY COUNTER-PHOBIC SIDE

At the end of my first Enneagram workshop, I found myself relating most deeply to the traits of a counter-phobic Type 6. A wave of embarrassment washed over me at the thought of acknowledging this new self-awareness in front of the group. It felt like a tender part of me was being revealed, exposing the quiet fears that had always governed my life.

On the surface, I projected an image of strength and independence—a cover for my underlying insecurities.

Speaking this truth was a crucial part of my healing process. By acknowledging these anxieties, I began to address and understand my core fears. I came to value the balance between my needs for independence and healthy attachments—I started to truly trust the meaningful connections in my life. This journey taught me that being vulnerable is not a weakness, but a path to finding my authentic wholeness.

In unpacking these nicknames, we find a spectrum of intricate traits. Let's deepen our understanding and empathy for each of them.

TYPE 6—TRUST

PERSONALITY TRAITS OF TYPE 6

Desire: To Feel Secure and Supported

At the core of your Type 6 is a longing for safety and security, both emotionally and physically. Speaking from my intimate experience with Type 6, I am convinced that our deepest longing is for an existential security—a kind that transcends both emotional and physical realms.

You lean on trusted individuals for guidance but remain watchful for potential pitfalls in relationships. You often find solace in beliefs or philosophies that provide a consistent framework for understanding life.

My drive to find stability in this chaotic world eventually led to a realization—the key isn't in trying to make everything predictable, but in anchoring myself deeply within the essence of true trust. This allowed me to embrace the ultimate uncertainty of life.

Emotion: Anxiety (Avoidance of Fear)

You strive to avoid the fear that governs the head center. While your tendency to dwell on scary scenarios may suggest that you are engaged with fear, you actually sidestep a direct encounter with it. Your mind races ceaselessly to stay one step ahead of fear, keeping the actual sensation just out of grasp.

While anxiety stands out as your primary emotion, you experience a depth of other feelings. Still, a constant sense of apprehension remains a familiar backdrop to your daily life.

Fixation: Anticipation of Threats

While your imagination is a powerful tool, it can lead you down the rabbit hole of worst-case scenarios. Imagine you're invited to a casual social gathering, maybe just coffee with a few friends. Instead of simply looking forward to a good time, your mind starts to wander into the territory of "what-ifs." What if I say something awkward? What if they ask a question I'm not prepared for? What if I have nothing to contribute to the conversation?

Your focus on these worst-case scenarios can become a self-fulfilling prophecy—your anxiety might lead you to act nervously, affecting your ability to engage in the conversation naturally.

This habit of constant worrying and doubting makes you hesitant and overly cautious. You end up second-guessing your decisions and seeking reassurance from others. This fixation on potential threats steals your present joy and inhibits your ability to fully participate in life.

Shadow: Projection

You commonly project your anxieties and insecurities onto others, leading to a hyper-vigilance of their motives—fearing their betrayal or abandonment. This can cause you to misconstrue innocent actions as potential threats, fostering tension and mistrust in relationships.

Let's say you're part of a group chat with friends, and suddenly you notice that the responses from a particular friend have become less frequent. Instead of considering various harmless reasons—maybe they're just busy or distracted—you begin to worry. You start to project your insecurities, thinking maybe they're ignoring you intentionally or they're talking about you behind your back. This mindset makes you hyper-aware and overly analytical of every message they do send, looking for hidden meanings or potential betrayal.

This cycle of projecting your anxieties onto others' simple actions fosters an atmosphere of tension and mistrust. In turn, your defensive behavior could make friends feel uneasy around you, reinforcing your initial fears and perpetuating a cycle of tension in your relationships. Your heightened vigilance often does more to create the fears you're trying to avoid rather than prevent them.

TYPE 6—TRUST

To free this pattern, connect with your universal trust, soften your desire for certainty, and embrace human fallibility. Create connection, vulnerability, and compassion in relationships, and approach human mistakes with an open mind.

MEET SARAH, WHO PROJECTED THE WORST

> Sarah, my client with the primary Type 6, was struggling in her marriage because of her deep-seated fear and mistrust. She was projecting her insecurities onto her husband, Tom, and interpreting his innocent actions as threats.
>
> Their relationship was marked with tension as her skepticism made her see Tom's natural human quirks as betrayals.
>
> So, we started using the Enneagram in our therapy sessions to help her understand the deeper reason she was seeking certainty and fearing betrayal so much. We focused our therapeutic journey on embodying the essence of universal trust.
>
> The turning point came when Tom arrived home late without calling. Instead of panicking, Sarah used her somatic practice to soothe her anxiety. She talked to Tom about how she was feeling, and that conversation was a beautiful catalyst.
>
> Since that transformative moment, their relationship has blossomed into a much healthier state. They've moved beyond the exhausting effort to always prove loyalty and now share a deeper connection rooted in vulnerability and compassion.

Sarah's journey illustrates the transformative power of cultivating inner trust. But what does Type 6 actually feel like from within? Let's

TYPE 6—TRUST

dive into the sensations and experiences of this type in your body, exploring the intricacies of both its personality and essence.

SOMATIC EXPERIENCE OF TYPE 6

Energetic Direction: Balanced

Compared to the other directions of your head—the Type 7 that turns outward or the Type 5 that turns inward—your Type 6 aims to balance or attune your inner thoughts and feelings with the outer world—especially with societal expectations. You want your beliefs to align with what's considered normal or right in your chosen group or culture.

For example, if you believe it's a good idea to question authority figures, but your community sees it as disrespectful or inappropriate, your Type 6 tendency might make you adjust how you express your questions, so you fit in. Alternatively, feeling out of sync might prompt you to find a different group or environment where your beliefs are more accepted or valued.

In Stress: Skepticism

Externally, there's a visible tension gripping your shoulders as you stand alert. Each breath is tinged with a palpable anticipation. Energy coils in the pit of your stomach, and your mind races, always plotting, always assessing. The echoing "what ifs" dominate your thoughts. With each perceived threat, the muscles of your neck tense up, and your heartbeat quickens in response.

The weight of responsibility sits heavy on your shoulders. Your gaze, discerning and sharp, constantly scans and evaluates. Every nuance, every hint of danger or inconsistency, captures your attention. Your fingers might twitch or clasp together, symbolizing a protective shield.

TYPE 6—TRUST

At the core, there's an ever-present craving, a need to feel that everything will be okay.

With Essence: Embodied Trust

Gradually, the tension in your body eases, and your stance becomes more relaxed. Your breathing deepens, becoming more rhythmic, as warmth replaces the coiled energy in your stomach. Thoughts become more deliberate, slowing down to a pace where trust begins to overshadow apprehension. Your heartbeat finds a steady, calm rhythm. Your discerning gaze softens, replacing vigilance with gentle curiosity. Open and relaxed, your fingers stretch out, signaling a newfound trust in your surroundings.

Rest in this calm state, and let this clarity carry you through our last section—the essence of a mature, trusting Type 6.

MATURE TYPE 6 — FIXATION TO ESSENCE

Without a doubt, helping your Type 6 grow and mature boils down to building this deep trust—in yourself, in others, and in life itself.

Imagine yourself as a mature oak tree standing tall—once you were a sapling swaying with every gust of wind, now you are deeply rooted and steadfast.

These strong roots represent your sense of inner security and trust in yourself. You stand firm, not because the wind has ceased, but because you have grown in wisdom and strength, understanding that true stability comes from within. This growth allows you to provide shelter and support to others, just as a mighty oak offers shade and refuge in the forest.

Remember all that insecurity and anxiety?

Rather than avoiding life's uncertainties, you now move through your days with confidence. Your old skepticism, tinged with cynicism, has matured into an open-minded curiosity, thanks to the trust you've anchored within.

Decisions feel different now. Gone are the days when you second-guess yourself all the time. Now, you're trusting yourself, leaning on your own intuition, making choices based on your own insights. You are no longer a prisoner to self-doubt, but a philosopher who questions the world with curiosity rather than fear.

And, what about your loyalty?

It used to be about safety in reciprocity, but now you're a source of reassurance for yourself and a support for those around you. This trust you've cultivated isn't just for you—it extends out to everyone you form bonds with.

You're still you, keeping things light with your humor, and your personality evokes trust and connection. It's your balanced approach—embracing fear as a natural energy and moving forward—that makes you truly brave.

That's quite the journey, wouldn't you agree?

With that, I'd love to end with more about my journey as a Type 6. Remember how I shared about that part of me that dreads the unknown? Now, I'll reveal how I found the inner courage to embrace those fears, discovering their nourishing essence along the way.

LIKE A GARDEN, MY PSYCHE HAS HIDDEN ROOTS

> Throughout my twenties, I was like a gardener tending to my inner landscape, carefully pruning and shaping its intricate paths. I was on a mission—to uproot every Type 6 fear and survival trait. But, like a garden, my psyche has hidden roots.
>
> A new decade was dawning, and I had diligently cultivated a

TYPE 6—TRUST

serene landscape within. But in an unexpected twist, a dark cloud cast over me—during a routine health procedure, a precancerous polyp was discovered growing inside me. For many, this would have been a fleeting concern. But for someone well acquainted with Type 6 tendencies, it was a life-threatening storm.

Suddenly, the garden I'd so carefully tended seemed under attack. Fears I thought I had weeded out rose again, consuming my mind with renewed vigor.

I spiraled.

My classic Type 6 fixations returned and I became an obsessed health detective—frantically connecting every possible dot between my lifestyle, nutrition, and potential risks. Craving reassurance, I turned outside myself, seeking a physician who'd share my concerns and walk alongside me. Yet, in this whirlwind of anxiety, I overlooked the truth grounded in the present.

The reality? My fears, intense as they were, hinged on shadows of the past. Yes, the polyp was precancerous, but it had been addressed effectively. Such is the nature of Type 6—spinning narratives so compelling that imagined threats loom larger than life. Yet, beneath my surface worry, a deeper layer began to surface.

I noticed a much deeper need to grapple with life's ultimate truth—mortality.

Once again, I turned to external sources, hoping to find a beacon in this existential journey. I wandered a maze of mystical and spiritual counsel—exploring traditions of meditation, yoga, psychedelics, and gurus of the East and West.

TYPE 6—TRUST

After a while, a clear insight emerged—my truest guide was not outside, but within.

So, I stepped away from endless advice and countless books—I embraced the art of simply being. I honed the skill of tuning in to my inner intuition, savoring those spontaneous moments of trust and clarity life throws our way.

For example, when I experienced strange sensations in my digestion, I resisted the urge to spiral into fears of cancer. Instead, I tapped into an inner knowing that the issue was harmless and an inner assurance that I would be okay, regardless of what happened next in life. Gradually, my fears began to mature, making room for a deeper engagement with the essence of life.

As I grew, the Enneagram did too, evolving from a basic tool to a profound guide.

Trust and inner guidance emerged as a key trait of my Type 6 experience. This inner wisdom also showed me that I wasn't just a single Enneagram type but had facets of all nine. This insight gave me the tools to more fully nourish my deep-seated anxieties.

Interestingly, I discovered that the essence of the *other* types provided potent nourishment for my Type 6 limitations. The strength of my Type 8 helped me step away from obsessive thoughts, the nurturance of my Type 2 embraced my inner worries, the discernment of my Type 1 bolstered my self-trust, and the richness of my Type 4 illuminated the deep love at the core of each fear. Embracing all these types within became my way forward.

TYPE 6—TRUST

I came to understand that my personality isn't a weed needing removal, but rather a sprout that needs help maturing.

The traits and anxieties I once sought to prune have matured into essential threads of my story, deserving of understanding and compassion. My personality, rich with nuance, now empowers me. The Type 6 within reminds me to savor the unpredictable dance of life and anchors me in what truly matters.

Every day is a chance to become a touch more human, more grounded, and more aligned with the world around us.

Thank you for accompanying me on this assuring journey. I hope my stories and insights have ignited deeper introspection within you.

Next, you'll find practical steps for embodying your Type 6 essence, designed to help you move beyond limiting personality traits and integrate this wisdom into your daily life. These resources are an *introduction* to the embodiment path — setting the stage for deeper explorations available in my full programs.

For a FREE printable copy of this embodiment guide for all 9 types, please visit my website: EnneagramofEssence.com

TYPE 6—TRUST

EMBODIMENT
PATH TO TRUST
EMBRACING TYPE 6 ESSENCE

JOURNEY INTO ESSENCE
The Enneagram of Essence's practical power is rooted in embodying essence and releasing limiting patterns. This brief guide to embodying Type 6's trust is my gift, setting the stage for a much deeper exploration available in my full programs.

ASSURANCE THROUGH TYPE 6 ESSENCE
Type 6 is my primary type, my north star. Its essence deeply nourishes me with an inner trust in life that resonates to my core. Even if it's not your primary, Type 6 offers a universal experience. *How could Type 6 essence enrich your inner and outer world?*

NATURE'S STABILITY
Consider the warmth of the sun on your face, a comforting and familiar presence that returns day after day. That's the reassuring spirit of Type 6.

MIND-BODY WELLNESS
Studies show that cultivating this kind of trust greatly affects your physiological state, enhancing your inner sense of safety and well-being.

© 2023 Enneagram of Essence. All rights reserved.

TYPE 6—TRUST

EMBODIMENT
PATH TO TRUST
EMBRACING TYPE 6 ESSENCE

STEP 1: IDENTIFY PORTALS TO TRUST

Identify what ignites feelings of assurance for you — nature, memories, reassuring people, etc. For me, stargazing and seeing the constellations' ancient patterns fills me with inner trust.

What symbols or experiences spark trust for you?

Incorporate elements like colors, textures, flavors, scents and sounds that mirror this quality into your space, as reminders of your Type 6 journey.

STEP 2: FEEL AND ANCHOR TRUST

Notice the distinct way stability and assurance feel within you. When I tap into this essence, I feel held and supported, like a leaf carried by a gentle stream, and my breathing naturally deepens.

What does stability feel like in your body?

Practice feeling and anchoring this essence deeply throughout your nervous system — visualize and feel it flow through you, influencing your posture, movements, and perceptions.

© 2023 Enneagram of Essence. All rights reserved.

EMBODIMENT
Path to Trust
EMBRACING TYPE 6 ESSENCE

STEP 3: CENTER TRUST

Make an effort to notice and value the essence of trust and stability in people around you. Focus on essence when noticing someone's personality.

Think about how centering essence could change your understanding and appreciation of people with the primary Type 6.

How could this practice deepen your understanding and connections with people primarily identified as Type 6?

STEP 4: CREATE A PRACTICE

Incorporate these steps into a flexible and creative practice, bringing it into your daily routine from a week to a month. Focus on portals that ignite trust and assurance. Through regular engagement, embodying true stability will become more and more effortless.

How will integrating these practices transform your daily life?

© 2023 Enneagram of Essence. All rights reserved.

TYPE 6—TRUST

EMBODIMENT
PATH TO TRUST
EMBRACING TYPE 6 ESSENCE

STEP 5: ABSTAIN FROM LIMITING TRAITS

Make space within yourself to cultivate trust. Type 6 personality traits serve as survival mechanisms so it's important to release them gently, leaning on inner resources for support.

Mindfully identify and release patterns that detract from your essence, including:

SEEKING EXTERNAL VALIDATION
Practice relying on your inner wisdom. View "mistakes" as opportunities to learn.

DOUBTING YOURSELF
Reinforce trust in yourself with affirmations — feel trust resonate within your body.

QUESTIONING AUTHORITY
Meet authority with empathy — shift from seeking external guidance to cultivating inner assurance.

SCANNING FOR DANGERS
Remain present. Bring your mind back to stability when anxiety about the future emerges.

IMAGINING THE WORST
Remember your current safety — envision scenes that reassure you.

© 2023 Enneagram of Essence. All rights reserved.

EMBODIMENT

PATH TO TRUST

EMBRACING TYPE 6 ESSENCE

STEP 5: ABSTAIN FROM LIMITING TRAITS

Mindfully identify and release patterns that detract from your essence, including:

BLAMING OTHERS FOR ANXIETIES

Take responsibility for your emotions, finding solace in practices that reinforce inner trust.

DISTRUSTING OTHERS

Embrace imperfection in humanity, focusing on recognizing the essence rather than flaws.

EXCESSIVE LOYALTY

Balance loyalty with self-care — set healthy boundaries and prioritize your well-being.

BEING SKEPTICAL

Address root fears with curiosity, continue to practice anchoring deep inner trust.

IGNORING INTERNAL GUIDANCE

Tune into and trust your intuition, strengthen internal guidance.

FOCUSING ON FEAR

Feel fear directly and let go of thoughts — ground yourself with physical sensations of support.

© 2023 Enneagram of Essence. All rights reserved.

TYPE 6—TRUST

> **EMBODIMENT**
> # PATH TO TRUST
> **EMBRACING TYPE 6 ESSENCE**

STEP 5: ABSTAIN FROM LIMITING TRAITS
Mindfully identify and release patterns that detract from your essence, including:

SEEKING EXTERNAL STABILITY
Accept life's inherent uncertainties, cultivating an inner stability that embraces the unknown.

TAKING ON TOO MUCH
Share responsibilities to distribute the load — let yourself feel supported by those around you.

OVER-PREPARING
Trust in your adaptability and resourcefulness, ground yourself and tap into inner strength.

Use Step 5 as a bridge, not fixed rules. By centering essence, your personality traits will naturally relax into the nourishing qualities of trust and assurance.

Let's conclude with a moment of integration through this guided meditation—opening the door to inner trust.

© 2023 Enneagram of Essence. All rights reserved.

TYPE 6—TRUST

GUIDED MEDITATION FOR TYPE 6

I encourage you to find a comfortable position, relax your body, and gently soften your focus. Read this slowly and with ease, twice—first to visualize the imagery, and then again to deeply connect with the sensations it evokes.

Relax your gaze.
Bring awareness into your body.

You are standing
underneath a vast starlit sky.

Feel the universe
wrapping you
in wonder.

The stars shimmer,
glowing beacons
of timeless guidance.

Their patterns mirrors
your inner knowing.

Breathe in the serenity
of the moon's warm light.

Around you,
whispers
of ancient constellations.

© 2023 Enneagram of Essence. All rights reserved.

TYPE 6—TRUST

GUIDED MEDITATION FOR TYPE 6

*Ageless formations,
protectors
of deep-seated trust.*

*Each star cluster,
a testament
to universal resilience.*

*Their light is steady.
Their stories are eternal.*

*Listen . . .
To the silent hum
of the cosmos.*

*Each twinkle,
a spark of
universal assurance.*

*Beneath your feet,
the earth grounds you.*

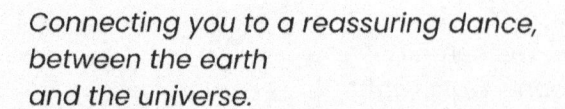

*Connecting you to a reassuring dance,
between the earth
and the universe.*

*Look up,
feel the vast expanse.*

© 2023 Enneagram of Essence. All rights reserved.

GUIDED MEDITATION FOR TYPE 6

*The cosmos recognizes
your search for stability.*

*Its immense depth,
a gentle embrace.*

*You're not just beneath the stars.
You're intertwined with them,
aligned with their eternal trust.*

Pause for a moment.

How did that meditation feel? Could you sense the vastness of the starry sky?

If that meditation resonated, it's because you accessed the spirit of trust, a quality that transcends external forms of life. The starry sky acts as a portal, but the assuring essence of Type 6 is inherently within you.

———(———

This is your journey. Absorb these suggestions at your pace—let them take root. When you're ready, turn the page and we'll explore the intricate tapestry of Type 5. Discover how to embrace true stillness and uncover silent wisdom.

© 2023 Enneagram of Essence. All rights reserved.

TYPE 5—CLARITY

WONDER & CURIOSITY

KEY ELEMENTS

- **Center**—Head, Wisdom, and Fear
- **Direction**—Inward Focus
- **Personality**—Observing Philosopher
- **Essence**—Clarity, Curiosity, Wonder

Do you ever find yourself...

- Compelled to understand life's deepest mysteries?
- Feeling like you lack the inner resources to engage in life?
- Retreating into your mind, observing from a bird's-eye view?

There is a facet of your personality that carries the cerebral depth of a Type 5. And even deeper, your inner essence resonates with its tranquil clarity.

TYPE 5—CLARITY

Have you ever felt...

- A quiet understanding beyond thought, deeper than words?
- A moment of clarity, where life's complexities seem simple?
- A sense of wonder that is independent from outside cues?

We all have a touch of the Type 5's intellectual curiosity—a mind that yearns to unravel life's enigmas. We all need a peaceful sanctuary, a quiet space to delve into our thoughts and perceive the stillness that lies beneath. The essence of this type serves as a doorway to a deep, serene knowing that transcends analytical processes.

Consider this a call to stop chasing wisdom through data and analysis.

Instead, nurture an inner stillness that values clarity and wonder beyond thought. By embracing this essence, you become an example of true wisdom and inner awareness in a world that is distracted by superficial knowledge. Let me tell you about the Type 5 part of me.

THAT PART OF ME THAT HIDES WITHIN MY MIND

> Although Type 5 isn't my dominant type, its thoughtful and inquisitive nature has always resonated within me. Whether you experience its traits sporadically, or identify with it as your core personality, I hope my experience will inspire you to explore and appreciate the Type 5 element within.
>
> For me, Type 5 emerges as an urge to retreat from the world and plunge into intellectual exploration, a pursuit that has captured much of my attention.
>
> In my early twenties, I was captivated by subjects about human nature—like anthropology, psychology, philosophy, and spirituality. I preferred the role of an observer, taking a bird's

TYPE 5—CLARITY

eye view rather than actively participating. Engrossed in texts and theories, I sought to understand the human condition academically, often bypassing real, emotional connections.

This analytical focus only intensified when I first engaged with the Enneagram.

Yet, I began to realize my pursuit of knowledge was both a haven and a hiding place. While I was deeply intrigued by what it means to be a human, this thirst of understanding was also a barrier against interacting with others emotionally.

In seeking to understand human life, I was actually avoiding it.

There was this lingering feeling that I lacked the inner resources to deal with everyday engagements—be it returning a phone call or attending a social gathering. This perceived inadequacy led me to retreat further into my intellectual safe spaces.

Does your quest for understanding ever distance you from personal connection? Does life ever feel like too much, leading you to perceive yourself as inadequate?

As I grew older, a thirst for real human connection emerged within me. This inner shift led me to the fields of counseling and therapy—realms rooted in empathy. I began to engage with life not just from my head but also from my heart and gut centers.

My relationship with Type 5 evolved. I've learned that true wisdom isn't just about accumulation—it's about discernment. Wisdom knows when to give and when to receive, when to analyze and when to feel, and most importantly, when to embrace the mystery.

I've come to appreciate the essence of wisdom that resides in moments of silence and the unknown—it's a wisdom that values not just answers but also the power of questions and the beauty of uncertainty.

My journey with Type 5 has truly reshaped my perspective. And while I'm eager to share all its details, there's a defining moment from my story I'll leave for the end of this chapter.

For now, let's get to know this intriguing personality and its enriching essence.

Take a moment.
Find your quiet place.
Prepare to dive in gently.

WELCOME TO TRUE CLARITY

To begin, let's connect with the essence of Type 5 within you. Picture a profound wonder residing in you—like a wide-eyed owl perched on a branch, quietly witnessing the forest. This wonder illuminates your mind and awakens your eyes with a childlike curiosity.

It's like having an insightful companion within you—an embodiment of clarity beyond thought, embracing life's answers and questions with equal wonder.

This curiosity is more than a characteristic to develop, it's an integral part of who you are. It's not solely about gathering data or facts—it's a natural state that emanates from deep inner stillness. An awareness that peers out at the world with a sense of clarity, finding depth and meaning in the mysterious nature of life.

TYPE 5—CLARITY

Imagine a simple walk in your neighborhood infused with the *essence* of curiosity. Instead of getting lost in a loop of analyzing and labeling each detail, you're deeply observing from a silent place. You feel a spacious, quiet connection with your surroundings. This brings a serene understanding, turning ordinary moments into gateways of wonder and clarity.

Isn't this a mystical facet of yourself?

You were born with a natural wonder that transcends thought, like a serene pond reflecting the sky. However, the obstacles of childhood clouded this essence, causing your Type 5 traits to kick into survival mode.

This led you to withdraw and seek refuge in privacy, searching for knowledge and understanding as a way to reconnect with your innate sense of clarity and wonder.

Because your essence is like pure emptiness—a state of clear seeing and inner witnessing—it can be perceived as a *lack* of inner resource or capability. In the face of life's intensity and demands, you began to experience your exquisite essence as a fragility.

Now, the Enneagram becomes your personal map—guiding you to embrace a wisdom that emanates from a source much deeper than your own thoughts or those of others. Embracing your authentic self means being able to engage in the world without all the answers.

Let's explore the fundamental relationship between the personality traits of Type 5 and its essence.

TYPE 5'S QUEST FOR CLARITY

Your Type 5 personality traits developed in response to stress, pulling your attention away from essence and into a state of fear and protection. You learned to seek your essence of clarity and wonder in external conditions—through analyzing and conserving energy.

This quest keeps you in a constant state of protectiveness and blinds you from recognizing the backdrop of serenity present in everyday life.

Consider my own experience. Instead of fully participating in life and connecting with people, I found myself observing and studying from the sidelines. This mindset limited my ability to form meaningful connections with others, and I missed out on the deeper insights that come from leaning into life. To heal my Type 5 tendencies, I had to learn to step out of my mental comfort zone and start experiencing life by actively engaging with it, rather than just analyzing it intellectually.

How have the times when you distanced from others limited the depth of your experiences?

Here's an Enneagram gem to ponder—every trait of the Observing Philosopher mirrors its essence. Your thirst for knowledge? It's a reflection of the universe's deep wisdom. Detachment? It's a sign of your inner yearning for real tranquility.

As we explore more, remember these traits are windows into a deeper desire—for the essence of clarity and quiet wisdom.

Take a moment to ponder these questions:

1. Do you ever need to detach from an area of your life? Why?
2. Do you ever yearn for solitude? What drives this need?
3. Do you ever seek knowledge over real-world engagement?
4. Do you ever feel incompetent and yearn to master an area of expertise?
5. Do you ever respond to anxiety by withdrawing and analyzing?
6. When did you last feel true clarity? Was it sparked by something outside or within you?

Allow these questions to linger in your awareness and return to explore them more fully. Let's trace back to where these patterns began—in childhood.

TYPE 5—CLARITY

CHILDHOOD OF TYPE 5 — ESSENCE TO FIXATION

Remembering your childhood through the lens of Type 5, you were quite the little intellectual.

While other kids were out playing in the sun, you could be found cozied up in the corner of the library—engrossed in a book about quantum physics or ancient civilizations. Or, you might have been navigating computer programs or diving deep into video game quests—preferring the world of information and ideas to that of physical activities and gatherings.

Life at home?

It was a self-contained place to dive deep into the mysteries of life and find some quiet. You found a little niche—a corner of your room or a tree in the backyard to retreat and restore.

In your community, you were the quiet observer, constantly analyzing. You chose your moments of engagement carefully, safeguarding your energy.

School was a mixed bag. You soaked up knowledge, but the traditional classroom wasn't your style—you've always liked to learn on your own terms. Your unconventional questions left teachers scratching their heads. Your curiosity, unquenchable.

Life for you was about understanding the world while preserving your limited inner resources. A delicate dance between introspection, curiosity, and energy conservation.

Your world might have seemed solitary to others, but for you, it was often an exciting universe of endless mysteries.

And yet, your curiosity as a Type 5 child was more a survival tool than your true essence. You *needed* to understand the world to feel safe in it. This excessive drive to grasp and analyze was your response to stress—a way to navigate the vast and often bewildering world around you.

TYPE 5—CLARITY

This is how the investigator in you took root. You learned the art of detachment, seeking understanding through observation and research. These traits grew with you, earning a few nicknames along the way. Let's unpack the traits of Type 5, beyond your formative years.

TYPE 5 NICKNAMES

The Investigator

You have a deep-rooted drive to understand the mechanics of the world—you are life's perpetual detective. Always digging, always questioning. While you might share your wealth of knowledge, your primary drive is to investigate and understand *for yourself*.

This quest for knowledge often leads you to rely on your own resources, valuing self-sufficiency in your intellectual pursuits. However, this can lead to a lonely isolation, as you often distance yourself from others in pursuit of your investigations.

The Observer

From a distance, you watch, quietly dissecting the world around you. This approach lets you grasp the bigger picture and the smaller details without becoming overwhelmed by emotional or energy-draining drama. Your analytical mind thrives in this space of observation, processing and understanding life from a safe remove.

Your quest for knowledge is voracious, but preserving your energy is just as vital. You feel unequipped to wade through life's overly-stimulating turbulence. So, there you are, finding comfort at the edge of the crowd, soaking up every detail with a keen, discerning eye.

The Philosopher

You have a love for deep philosophical thought, an endless wonder that reaches for the stars. Drawn to the profound questions of

TYPE 5—CLARITY

existence, you often dwell on topics others overlook. This nickname captures your urge to venture beyond the superficial, seeking truths that illuminate the very core of existence.

Your quest isn't just for knowledge but for an integrated understanding, a synthesis of insights that connects the dots of life's mysteries. For you, understanding is the bridge that connects you to others and the tapestry of life. However, at times, your relentless pursuit of these deep questions may lead you to overanalyze or become overly introspective, potentially distancing you from the simple joys of life and more practical, immediate concerns.

MEET KEN, A TRUE OBSERVER WHO LIVED IN A TENT OF SOLITUDE

> I will always have a place in my heart for Ken, the quintessential Type 5. I'll never forget that summer he moved into a tent in my uncle's backyard. For Ken, it was a way to unplug from life's hustle and embrace a life of simplicity.
>
> He was drawn to a mystical path that favored solitude—one that whispered wisdom in silence rather than amidst the chatter of the world. Ken didn't see himself as running away—he was tuning in, creating a bubble where he could engage with life on his own terms.
>
> Let me tell you, that modest tent was more than just shelter—it was his gateway to realms of profound wisdom and imagination. With books borrowed from the local library, he'd spend hours engrossed in their pages. From spirituality to history, quantum physics, and fantasy—he delved deep into every subject he encountered.
>
> But he didn't just hoard words—he spun them into tales too. He was a gifted writer. In the hushed serenity of his backyard

oasis, he weaved intricate stories, spun verses of poetry that danced between the profound and the whimsical.

He was a true observer, living on the outskirts of life, but peering in with an insight that was nothing short of beautiful.

I offer Ken's story as a clear reflection of someone with a primary Type 5. It's a contrast to my own journey of retreating into my mind, curbing my true potential and authenticity. At that point in his life, Ken wasn't drawn to uncover his other centers or facets. For him, the role of an observer, deeply rooted in thought, was both rich and rewarding.

Every journey is unique—sometimes you lean deeply into your primary type, other times you may feel a pull to awaken another facet of yourself. There will also be moments urging you to explore the full spectrum. I encourage you to listen to your inner voice and remain receptive to evolving ways of using the wisdom of the Enneagram.

As each of these nicknames are packed with important traits, let's delve into them with the same meticulous care a Type 5 would offer.

PERSONALITY TRAITS OF TYPE 5

Desire: To Feel Capable and Competent

Your personality is rooted in an intense longing to comprehend and make sense of the vast world. This yearning doesn't stem from curiosity alone—it is intertwined with a primal fear of helplessness, inadequacy, or incapability. In your quest to counter these vulnerabilities, you strive to acquire enough knowledge and skills to feel secure and confident in your ability to handle life's challenges.

This drive for knowledge leads you to become an expert in specific areas of interest. Your specialized knowledge, your reservoir of facts and insights, becomes a shield—a protective barrier against being incapable or incompetent in life.

TYPE 5—CLARITY

Emotion: Detachment (Internalized Fear)

Your emotional landscape is like an onion—layered and complex. On the surface, you appear detached, withdrawing to prevent the world from overwhelming you. But beneath this aloof exterior lies a whirlwind of anxiety. Faced with a world that seems massive and chaotic, your instinct is to retreat, seeking refuge within the depths of your inner mind.

It's worth noting that beneath your seemingly calm exterior, there is a storm of intellectual and emotional activity. Contrary to popular belief, you also hold the emotions of the heart—sadness, loneliness, deep love. However, these feelings often stay hidden, kept as a closely guarded secret, sometimes shared only with those you trust enough to glimpse the intricate layers of your inner world.

Fixation: Avarice

Not in the way you might think. Your avarice is not a simple greed for material things—it's a deeper yearning for knowledge, time, and space. A sense that there's never quite enough. This feeling drives you to gather information, to "hoard" your resources, to pull back and safeguard your emotional and intellectual energy.

Within you, there's a relentless need to be prepared, to ensure that you're never found intellectually lacking or ill-equipped. As you retreat into your own world, it becomes a fortress, where you feel protected from the demands and drains of the external world.

Shadow: Depletion

Hidden within you is a constant sense of potential depletion, and this is where the shadow of avarice truly shows its face. You fear that engaging too deeply with the world might leave you emptied out, overwhelmed, or vulnerable. This shadowed form of avarice urges you to withhold—to guard your thoughts, feelings, and energy fiercely.

TYPE 5—CLARITY

By recognizing this shadow and understanding how it fuels your hunger for information, you can come to see that your innate wonder and curiosity are sources of resilience and capability, rather than vulnerabilities. Your questions bring as much to the table as all your answers. Embracing these qualities enables a deeper and more fulfilling connection with the world around you, without the need for all the answers.

MEET SALLY, ALWAYS CURIOUS—PERPETUALLY SEEKING

My client Sally's mind was always "on" like a whirlwind of questions—always seeking, always learning. Each question she posed reflected her deep yearning—to comprehend, to feel capable, all while tethered by a current of anxiety.

As we delved deeper in our sessions, it became clear—Sally was yearning for more than just knowledge from the external world. She was reaching for a connection to something larger, a cosmic understanding beyond the bounds of logical thought.

And here's where things really clicked for Sally. During our exploration of the Path of Nourishment, a revelation unfolded. It dawned on her that the answers weren't always outside, or even in thought. That profound well of stillness, that ageless wisdom? It was within her, patiently waiting, hoping she'd tune in.

By anchoring herself in the quiet wisdom—the "field" of stillness around her thoughts—Sally learned she didn't need to reach outwards for knowledge to feel competent. She could lean into her own inner stillness, her connection to a deeper knowing. Bit by bit, she began to let go of the need to understand everything, finding she could be fully competent in her own innate way.

TYPE 5—CLARITY

> Sally remains intensely curious and still loves learning—however, her curiosity now arises from a place of pure fascination and joy rather than a *need* for safety and competence in the world.

Sally's transformation serves as a beacon for the Type 5 in each of us. But what does Type 5 actually feel like from within? Let's dive into the sensations and experiences of this type in your body, exploring the intricacies of both its personality and essence.

SOMATIC EXPERIENCE OF TYPE 5

Energetic Direction: Inward

Compared to the other head types—the Type 7 that turns outward or the Type 6 that balances—your Type 5 turns inward, immersing in the reservoir of knowledge and insight within. You are drawn inward, to deeply analyze and intellectually comprehend the complexities of the outer world.

For instance, when faced with an external problem, you turn inward, spending hours delving into research and prioritizing a comprehensive grasp of the issue over quick, practical solutions. During discussions, you prefer to remain contemplative, emphasizing deep insight and understanding over active contribution or engagement.

In Stress: The Observer

On the surface, you seem calm, stoic. Inside, there's a constant hum of alertness. Like a detective, you're always scanning, noticing without external response. Your breath feels shallow, a sign of the mind racing to gather, analyze, and store information. A weight sits in your chest, hinting at feeling unequipped for what life will throw at you next.

TYPE 5—CLARITY

Tightness lingers in your temples and neck, as if bracing for the next puzzle.

You're on edge, always set to "observe and compute". This constant need to decipher life's complexities often leaves you exhausted and lacking the energy to simply enjoy the moment.

With Essence: Embodied Wisdom

As the pressure of needing to understand relaxes, a nourishing sense of wonder sets in.

Inside, there's a quiet that's tangible, like the stillness of a serene lake. Each breath is deep and steady, bringing a sense of clarity. You feel as if a weight of overthinking has been lifted. Your heart beats calmly, echoing a tranquility that feels familiar and comforting. You're connected to a calm wisdom that's always been there, waiting for you to notice. You're simply present, taking in life's moments with gentle, spontaneous understanding.

Embrace this essential stillness as we delve into our last section and get to know the mature Type 5.

MATURE TYPE 5 — FIXATION TO ESSENCE

Your Type 5 matures when you transition from seeking knowledge as proof of expertise to embracing your true competence, which flows from quiet wisdom.

Picture yourself as a wise owl perched in the heart of an ancient forest. In your earlier days, your mind was sharp and analytical, like a keen hunter. But now, you've evolved into a peaceful witness, brimming with wonder and a natural clarity that arises from simply being present—observing the forest without the need for analysis.

Remember your need for privacy and preserving your inner resources?

You've discovered a wellspring of inner clarity that never runs dry. Rather than depending on detachment, you embrace genuine

TYPE 5—CLARITY

connections, engaging with others without reservation. Your understanding extends beyond the world to encompass people and their emotions as well.

And what about your avarice?

It's shifted from a fixation on hoarding knowledge to a deep appreciation for the mysteries of life. You've come to recognize that there is a profound wisdom in embracing the unknown and undefined. Now, wonder and curiosity are sources of nourishment rather than tools to acquire more. You share wisdom, not out of a need to prove yourself, but out of a genuine desire to connect and inspire.

You're still you though, your introspective nature shining a light on hidden truths, your pursuit of understanding offering clarity in a world of chaos. It's your discerning approach—seeking knowledge while respecting the mysteries of life—that truly defines your maturity.

That's an enriching process, don't you think?

With that, I'm excited to end by sharing more about my Type 5 journey—remember when I told you about the time I stepped back from the world and hid behind my academic studies? Now I'll tell you about that pivotal moment when I learned how to use my Type 5 essence as a bridge to deeper connection and clarity.

I FELT MORE COMPETENT STUDYING PEOPLE THAN CONNECTING WITH THEM

> In my early twenties you could find me hunkered down in the stacks of my university library, pouring over textbooks that explored the intricacies of human behavior. I was intoxicated by the abstract intellectuality of cultural anthropology, gripped by its objective lens on humanity, and drawn to the intricacies of the human condition.

TYPE 5—CLARITY

Like a Type 5, I found solace and competence in the observer role.

My world was dominated by the cerebral. I was scared to form new connections and I found refuge and passion in knowledge. My relationships were with theories and not people—my emotions were studied, not shared.

I truly cared about people, yet I was intimidated by them, so I viewed humanity as a subject to be studied.

As the seasons of life turned, a shift happened within me, an unfurling. My interest in human behavior began to morph into something more intimate. I felt a pull, a yearning to understand not just the mechanics of human behavior but the direct, visceral experience of it.

This shift became more evident when I delved into psychology. The intellectual appeal was undeniable, yet it was not enough. I still felt as if I was studying humanity through a glass pane—a distance that once felt protective began to feel limiting.

It was the Enneagram that helped me realize that hiding within my pursuit of knowledge was my shadow of incompetence—I was afraid of my heart center and the humanity that I belonged to. The idea of not just observing but interacting and empathizing began to have appeal.

This was a new direction, a much-needed journey into my own heart. So, I pivoted—from theoretical musings to the enriching realm of counseling and therapy.

I still see traces of my Type 5 trappings. When I find myself stepping back into the observer's role and intellectualizing the

TYPE 5—CLARITY

experiences of my clients, friends, or family members, I remember the essence of Type 5.

Guided by its quiet wisdom, I have learned to soothe the sharp scrutiny of my mind. Instead, I immerse in the present, soothe my fear of depletion, and relax into the silence of the unknown and undefined.

Ironically, embodying the wisdom of Type 5 has guided my journey to wholeness. It's taught me that life is more than just watching from the sidelines, it's about living, becoming, and integrating all three centers—head, heart, and gut.

Thank you for accompanying me on this serene journey. I hope my stories and insights have ignited deeper introspection within you.

Next, you'll find practical steps for embodying your Type 5 essence, designed to help you move beyond limiting personality traits and integrate this wisdom into your daily life. These resources are an *introduction* to the embodiment path — setting the stage for deeper explorations available in my full programs.

For a FREE printable copy of this embodiment guide for all 9 types, please visit my website: EnneagramofEssence.com

TYPE 5—CLARITY

Embodiment
Path to Wonder
Embracing Type 5 Essence

Journey into Essence
The Enneagram of Essence's practical power is rooted in embodying essence and releasing limiting patterns. This brief guide to embodying Type 5's wonder is my gift, setting the stage for a much deeper exploration available in my full programs.

Peace Through Type 5 Essence
Even though Type 5 is not my primary type, its essence brings peace and wonder to my life. It calms my mind with a quiet stillness, fostering mental tranquility and soothing my interactions in the world. *How could Type 5 essence enrich your inner and outer world?*

Nature's Stillness
Consider the quiet clarity and wonder that dawns on you in the stillness of the forest, where each step brings an inner tranquility. That's the serene spirit of Type 5.

Mind-Body Wellness
Studies show this kind of peaceful engagement can soften your stress responses, fostering a gentle, mindful presence within.

© 2023 Enneagram of Essence. All rights reserved.

TYPE 5—CLARITY

EMBODIMENT
PATH TO WONDER
EMBRACING TYPE 5 ESSENCE

STEP 1: IDENTIFY PORTALS TO WONDER

Identify what ignites feelings of quiet clarity for you — nature, memories, peaceful people, etc. For me, visualizing the tranquil forest, the silent presence of trees, ignites a serene sense of wonder.

What symbols or experiences spark wonder for you?

Incorporate elements like colors, textures, flavors, scents and sounds that mirror this quality into your space, as reminders of your Type 5 journey.

STEP 2: FEEL AND ANCHOR WONDER

Notice the distinct way clarity and wonder feel within you. When I tap into this essence, my mind becomes still, light, and expansive, often bringing a cool, soothing sensation to my brain.

What does quiet clarity feel like in your body?

Practice feeling and anchoring this essence deeply throughout your nervous system — visualize and feel it flow through you, influencing your posture, movements, and perceptions.

© 2023 Enneagram of Essence. All rights reserved.

Embodiment
Path to Wonder
Embracing Type 5 Essence

Step 3: Center Wonder

Make an effort to notice and value the essence of clarity and wonder in people around you. Focus on essence when noticing someone's personality.

Think about how centering essence could change your understanding and appreciation of people with the primary Type 5.

How could this practice deepen your understanding and connections with people primarily identified as Type 5?

Step 4: Create a Practice

Incorporate these steps into a flexible and creative practice, bringing it into your daily routine from a week to a month. Focus on portals that ignite wonder and clarity. Through regular engagement, embodying true curiosity will become more and more effortless.

How will integrating these practices transform your daily life?

© 2023 Enneagram of Essence. All rights reserved.

Embodiment
Path to Wonder
Embracing Type 5 Essence

Step 5: Abstain from Limiting Traits

Make space within yourself to cultivate clarity. Type 5 personality traits serve as survival mechanisms so it's important to release them gently, leaning on inner resources for support.

Mindfully identify and release Type 5 patterns that detract from your essence, including:

Pressured Pursuit of Knowledge
Balance learning with embracing the unknown. Let curiosity lead without pressure.

Social Withdrawal
Blend solitude with meaningful social interactions. Find solace in both alone time and shared moments.

Guarding Inner Resources
Share your knowledge and wisdom. Recognize that your inner resources are abundant.

Emotional Detachment
Engage with your emotions as paths to insight. Explore feelings with curiosity.

Neglecting Physical Well-being
Attune to your body with curiosity and care.

© 2023 Enneagram of Essence. All rights reserved.

EMBODIMENT
PATH TO WONDER
EMBRACING TYPE 5 ESSENCE

STEP 5: ABSTAIN FROM LIMITING TRAITS
Mindfully identify and release Type 5 patterns that detract from your essence, including:

FIERCE INDEPENDENCE
Foster connections and embrace interdependence. Recognize the strength in shared experiences.

DECISION PARALYSIS
Balance logic with intuition. Accept the imperfection in choices.

GUARDING PRIVACY
Gradually open up to others. Find safety in vulnerability.

FEAR OF INCOMPETENCE
Trust in your ability to learn and adapt. View challenges as opportunities for growth.

SOCIAL AVOIDANCE
View interactions as enriching, not invasive. Embrace a balanced engagement with life.

RIGID ROUTINE
Trust that your essence is sufficient for new experiences.

© 2023 Enneagram of Essence. All rights reserved.

TYPE 5—CLARITY

EMBODIMENT
PATH TO WONDER
EMBRACING TYPE 5 ESSENCE

STEP 5: ABSTAIN FROM LIMITING TRAITS

Mindfully identify and release Type 5 patterns that detract from your essence, including:

SKEPTICISM AND CYNICISM

Cultivate optimism and trust. Challenge negative viewpoints and embrace risk with self-assurance.

SUPPRESSING EMOTIONS AND NEED

Communicate openly with trusted friends. Approach vulnerability with curiosity.

AVOIDING ESSENTIAL TASKS

See tasks as growth opportunities. Stay nourished by your inner clarity when you work on a draining task.

Use Step 5 as a bridge, not fixed rules. By centering essence, your personality traits will naturally relax into the nourishing qualities of clarity and wonder.

Let's conclude with a moment of integration through this guided meditation—opening the door to inner clarity.

© 2023 Enneagram of Essence. All rights reserved.

GUIDED MEDITATION FOR TYPE 5

I encourage you to find a comfortable position, relax your body, and gently soften your focus. Read this slowly and with ease, twice—first to visualize the imagery, and then again to deeply connect with the sensations it evokes.

Relax your eyes.
Take a deep, calming breath in.

You're at the entrance
of an ancient forest.

A cool, gentle breeze
touches your face.

Inhale the aroma
of earth and leaves.

Around you,
the knowing presence
of ancient trees.

Wise giants.
Guardians
of quiet wonder.

Each tree stands,
with centuries
of tranquil knowing.

© 2023 Enneagram of Essence. All rights reserved.

TYPE 5—CLARITY

GUIDED MEDITATION FOR TYPE 5

*Their roots deep,
their wisdom, even deeper.*

*Listen . . .
Whispers of rustling leaves.
Distant bird calls.*

*Each sound,
a note of the forest's wonder.*

*Sunlight dances
through the canopy above.*

*Golden patterns on the ground,
secrets for forest wanderers.*

*Reach out,
touch the bark.*

*Rough, textured tales
of years gone by.*

*You walk deeper.
Stillness envelops you.*

*The forest recognizes
your quest for clarity.*

© 2023 Enneagram of Essence. All rights reserved.

TYPE 5—CLARITY

GUIDED MEDITATION FOR TYPE 5

You're not just in the forest.
You're a part of it,
absorbing its silent wisdom.

Pause for a moment.

How did that meditation feel? Could you sense the silence of the ancient forest?

If that meditation resonated, it's because you accessed the *spirit* of clarity, which is beyond external forms of life. The quiet forest acts as a portal, yet true clarity and quiet awareness is an internal, intrinsic part of you.

This is your journey. Absorb these suggestions at your pace—let them take root. As you turn the page, we'll begin our journey into your heart center, delving into the core of your emotions and the essence of love that connects us all.

© 2023 Enneagram of Essence. All rights reserved.

TYPE 5—CLARITY

WANT TO DEEPEN YOUR ENNEAGRAM ESSENCE JOURNEY?

Visit: EnneagramofEssence.com

You'll discover a wealth of resources designed to support wherever you are on the Enneagram path — explore our free resources, fundamentals course, podcasts, workshops, and a full accredited certification program.

YOUR HEART CENTER

HAVEN OF YOUR HEART

LOVE & SADNESS

Have you ever experienced your heart center...

- As a warm "depth" or "fullness" in your chest?
- As a tenderness around, yet beyond, your passing emotions?
- As the love that embraces all your feelings and desires?

Take a moment to reflect.
Place your hands gently on your chest.
Sense into this center of your being.

Ponder these questions, letting insights emerge naturally:

1. Which emotions most often arise in your heart?
2. What do these emotions feel like? Are they subtle or all-consuming?
3. How does the space of your heart differ from these passing emotions?
4. What sensations arise when you tap into the love of your heart center?

5. Are there specific moments when you really feel this loving awareness?
6. What words describe this space—the *essence* of your heart center?

Allow these questions to linger in your awareness, giving yourself the time and space to explore them fully.

HEART CENTER ESSENCE — LOVE

The essence of your heart center is love—a quality that transcends your fleeting emotions. It is a resonant warmth that fills your heart, transforming it into a nurturing hearth where compassion, worth, and beauty flourish.

This love radiates from your chest, embracing your emotions, desires, and relationships. It's a sanctuary where love extends beyond emotion —a source of universal kindness, acceptance, and belonging.

HEART CENTER EMOTION — SADNESS

Your Heart Center is also the realm where you navigate the heavy waters of sadness and its relatives—grief and melancholy. These tender emotions can feel like deep waters, pulling you down and drowning your sense of connection and belonging. They can make you feel isolated and overwhelmed—weighing down your capacity for love.

However, when acknowledged and embraced, sadness transforms into a bridge—leading you back to a nourishing experience of love.

Think of sadness as a passing wave in the boundless sea of your inner love. Met with awareness and gentle acceptance, these waves recede, revealing the warm depths of your inherent love. Through practice, you can come to understand that this vast ocean is always present, spacious enough to hold your sorrows yet never overwhelmed by them.

I invite you to redefine your relationship with sadness. While it can feel like a burden, it's also a portal to deep empathy and reconnects you to the loving core of your heart center.

HEART CENTER PERCEPTION — EMOTIONAL

In this space, emotions are not just feelings but lenses through which you view the world. Here you sense the nuances of empathy and gauge emotional undercurrents in relationships. Your own self-image and self-worth take form as you interact emotionally with your environment. It's the realm where your feelings translate into a deeper understanding of your needs and desires.

HEART CENTER SEEKS — APPRECIATION

This is the center of your emotional objectives and goals. Here you find what your heart values and actively pursue it. This includes striving for meaningful relationships, longing for appreciation, and seeking a sense of belonging. It's also where you focus on self-improvement practices, from enhancing your self-esteem to nurturing deeper emotional connections through vulnerability and compassion.

HEART CENTER ENERGETIC DIRECTIONS

Type 4 (Inward): Your focus turns inward—deep into your heart for introspection. Here, desires are used to express authenticity and sadness is honed to create identity and beauty.

Type 3 (Balanced): Your attention is balanced—aligning your heart's expression with the values of the outer world. Sadness serves as a catalyst for ambition and desire fuels achievement.

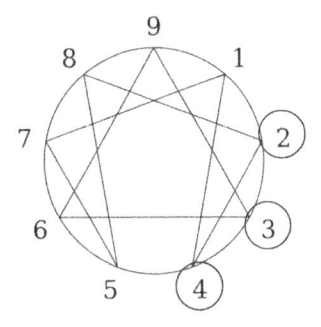

Type 2 (Outward): Your attention turns outward—toward the world for connection and engagement. Desires are channeled into acts of kindness and sadness is used as the bedrock for compassion and care.

HEART CENTER PRACTICES AND TRADITIONS

There are many cultural traditions and spiritual practices that emphasize the realm of the heart, love, and emotions. Here are just a few examples.

Yogic traditions, such as Bhakti yoga, emphasize opening the heart and cultivating love through asanas that awaken the heart chakra. Similarly, the Loving-kindness meditation, rooted in Buddhist practice, involves sending love and well wishes toward ourselves and then to loved ones, acquaintances, strangers, and even those we have conflicts with.

Wellness practices like gratitude journaling or heart-centered breathing can amplify feelings of love, appreciation, and emotional connection. There's a warm embrace in practices that cater to the heart, bringing us closer to each other and the world around us.

Examples:

- Bhakti yoga
- Loving-kindness meditation
- Gratitude journaling
- Heart-centered breathing
- Prayers of the Heart

With this foundation for your heart center, let's conclude this chapter with a guided meditation. Immerse yourself in this portal into the essence of this center, the haven of your heart.

HEART CENTER MEDITATION

I encourage you to find a comfortable position, relax your body, and gently soften your focus. Read this slowly and with ease, twice—first to visualize the imagery, and then again to deeply connect with the sensations it evokes.

Draw in a deep, nourishing breath.
Tune in to your heart center.

Feel the sensations of your chest,
the rhythm of your breath and heart.
Find the space behind your ribs.

Notice any tension.
Tenderly invite it to relax.

Notice the ebb and flow of your emotions,
signaling your needs and desires.

Imagine your heart as the deep ocean,
warm, embracing, and boundless.

Within this vast water,
emotions rise like waves,
shaping your surface.

Each emotion is distinct.
Each emotion is temporary.

HEART CENTER MEDITATION

*Beneath these shifting currents,
is an ever-present,
nurturing love.*

*Notice . . .
Most of the ocean of your heart
is warm, full, embracing.*

*Radiant, kind, worthy.
Full of compassion,
value, and belonging.*

*Feel its presence as a soothing warmth,
an embrace that's always there,
ready to guide and nourish you.*

Pause for a moment.

How did that meditation feel? Did you experience the warm "ocean" of your heart?

If that meditation resonated, it's because you tapped into the haven of your heart—the warm tenderness beyond your passing emotions. Remember, you do not need to cease your emotions in order to sense the nourishment of your heart center.

HEART CENTER MEDITATION

With this foundation, let's explore the expressions of your heart center across its three types, beginning with the deep intimate love of Type 4, where beauty and belonging interweave.

TYPE 4—BELONGING

RADIANT BEAUTY & AUTHENTICITY

KEY ELEMENTS

- **Center**—Heart, Love, & Sadness
- **Direction**—Inward Focus
- **Personality**—Romantic Individualist
- **Essence**—Belonging, Authenticity, Inner Beauty

Do you ever find yourself...

- Feeling a strong pull to express your uniqueness?
- Feeling melancholy when life falls short of your vivid dreams?
- Sensing that everyone else belongs, while you're left out of the connection?

There is a facet of your personality that carries the emotional intensity and uniqueness of a Type 4. And even deeper, your essence holds its radiant nourishment.

TYPE 4—BELONGING

Have you ever felt...

- Intimately close to life while listening to a moving song?
- Truly seen and appreciated when sharing a personal story?
- A deep sense of belonging in a moment of artistic inspiration?

Within each of us is a deep Type 4 essence—a heart that longs for true belonging, authenticity, and depth in a world that often feels shallow. This essence is your doorway to true belonging within the rich tapestry of life.

Consider this a call to stop longing for what's missing and idealized.

Instead, find radiance in the ordinary and cultivate a depth of connection that doesn't rely on the extraordinary. By doing this, you become an example of inner belonging and authenticity in a world obsessed with *looking* unique. Let me tell you about the Type 4 part of me.

THAT PART OF ME THAT LIVES IN DEEP FANTASY

> Although Type 4 is not my main type, its intensity draws me into my depths all the time. Whether you feel the pull of Type 4 only now and then or as the driving force of your primary type, I hope my story helps you recognize your own.
>
> Within me, Type 4 often emerges as a romantic nostalgia for my hometown. It's not just a simple longing for the streets where I played as a child, but a deep, poignant ache for a time and feeling that's slipped away.
>
> This emotional draw to the past has led me to reflect on *where* to find my true sense of belonging.

TYPE 4—BELONGING

This nostalgia spins romantic daydreams about my hometown, which is puzzling. I cherish my current home in the mystical mountains of Western North Carolina, and I don't long for the muggy town in North Florida where I grew up.

Through exploring the essence of Type 4, I've come to a powerful realization. My longing for home isn't tied to a physical location—it's a deeper quest for inner connection—a sense of true belonging that bonds me with the universe itself.

I'm excited to explore my Type 4 journey further with you and I saved a special part for the end of this chapter. For now, let's get into the traits of this radiant personality type.

So, take a deep breath.
Settle into your heart.
Get ready to immerse deeply.

WELCOME TO TRUE BELONGING

Let's begin by tuning into the radiant essence of Type 4 that already resides within you. Imagine a deeply resonant, yet gentle melody playing from within your heart—a feeling of belonging that's always available, within your own presence.

It's as if a timeless poet dwells within you, embodying a depth of emotion and beauty that lingers like a haunting sonnet long after it's been recited.

Picture yourself in a state where belonging doesn't come from an external source, but is a foundational aspect of who you are. This inner sense of connection isn't tied to certain people or relationships—it's an ever-present feeling that emanates from your very heart.

TYPE 4—BELONGING

Imagine being in a group where everyone else appears to be well-acquainted. Instead of feeling like an outsider, you experience a natural warmth and openness. This comfort arises from a deep-rooted sense of belonging within you, a feeling of being at home in the world. This inner grounding empowers you to engage openly, enabling you to feel at ease and connected, even in a group where everyone else seems closely knit.

When you radiate a warmth that makes others feel welcome, you foster an environment that mirrors connection back to you.

It's an intimate path worth joining, wouldn't you say?

You came into this world in a natural state of belonging, feeling completely at home within yourself and the world. Yet, life's challenges led you to drift away from this inner connection, nudging your Type 4 into survival mode.

This disconnect led you to develop painful traits like longing and melancholy, setting you on a ceaseless search for a true sense of belonging.

This is where the Enneagram offers a soothing hand. It acts like a compass, guiding you out of emotional survival mode and back to your inherent sense of intimacy with life itself. It helps you understand that your emotional burdens are signs of your deeper yearning to reconnect with your essence.

Let's unpack the fundamental relationship between the essence of Type 4 and its personality traits.

TYPE 4'S QUEST FOR BELONGING

Your Type 4 traits emerged as a response to stress, shifting your focus from essence to a state of longing and fantasy. As a result, you started to pursue a sense of belonging by seeking uniqueness in relationships and personal identity.

TYPE 4—BELONGING

This quest keeps you in a constant state of melancholy and sadness, obscuring the depth of connections already present in your world.

Consider my own Type 4 experience. My nostalgia for my hometown often overshadows the beauty of my current surroundings. My romanticized view of the past keeps me from fully connecting with my present life. Dwelling in memories diminishes my appreciation of what's here now—my growing friendships and the welcoming warmth of this mountain community.

Has romanticizing the past or dwelling in nostalgic fantasy ever blocked your ability to appreciate the present?

Here's a provocative insight—every trait of the Romantic-Individualist reflects its core essence. Your pursuit of uniqueness and profound emotional depth mirrors the inherent radiance of life. Your desire for an extraordinary, external connection marks a deeper yearning for a radiant belonging that originates from within.

As we examine these traits in the next section, reflect on how they each hint at a deeper yearning for inner belonging, radiance, and authenticity.

Take a moment to ponder these questions:

1. Are there aspects of your life that feel too shallow? Do you crave depth?
2. Do you ever yearn to be unique or even special? Why?
3. Does your attention ever pull deep into the inner emotions of your heart?
4. Do you ever respond to grief by withdrawing deeper into sadness?
5. Where do you find beauty—in the extraordinary or the ordinary?
6. When did you last feel true belonging? Was it sparked by something outside or within you?

TYPE 4—BELONGING

Allow these questions to linger and return to explore them more fully. Now, we'll journey back to early childhood—to the time when your Type 4 characteristics first appeared.

CHILDHOOD OF TYPE 4 — ESSENCE TO FIXATION

Reflecting on your childhood, through the lens of Type 4, do you remember feeling the world more deeply than others?

You often found yourself standing apart, perceiving life in vivid hues while many seemed content in shades of gray. You were left with the impression that your rich emotional landscape was what defined you.

You were a child filled with emotion and artistic inclinations. Did you find yourself sketching imaginary worlds or humming your own tunes? These were your outlets for the emotional storm that was always swelling inside you.

And what about your childhood room?

It was a sanctuary of beauty, a place filled with knick-knacks and art that reflected your unique style and depth.

But, woven into these memories is a thread of melancholy. You always felt like something was missing—an ideal reality was always just beyond your grasp. As you grew, this sentiment tinted your world, casting you as the eternal outsider.

Did you ever feel misread or misinterpreted?

Moments of feeling unseen intensified this sentiment, igniting a deep desire to be truly recognized—to have your rich emotions and distinct perspectives embraced.

Your sense of unique authenticity grew out of those early instances where you felt sidelined. Under stress, romantic longing became your coping mechanism—a strategy to deal with a world that seemed unaccepting.

TYPE 4—BELONGING

Now, let's progress into adulthood and explore the rich nuances of the Romantic-Individualist's personality.

TYPE 4 NICKNAMES

The Individualist

Growing up, you felt like the puzzle piece that didn't quite fit, sparking an intense quest for authenticity and identity. Instead of trying to blend in, you leaned into your unique traits, seeing mainstream expectations as suffocating.

This isn't a mere urge to stand out or rebel.

It's a deep-rooted need for authenticity, born from moments of questioning your belonging in the world. It's not about being defiant but about seeking true recognition and escaping the shadow of feeling unimportant.

The Artist

Your identity is deeply rooted in creativity and self-expression. Every aspect of your life becomes a creation—a window into your intense emotions and vivid inner universe. Intuitive and imaginative, you constantly delve into your feelings, translating their unique shades into something real. This not only helps you understand yourself but also connect with others.

Your authentic flair makes your stories resonate deeply, adding depth and richness to your life and the lives you touch. While there's an underlying fear of being overlooked, when you truly embrace your essence, your creativity blooms, becoming a pure reflection of your depth.

TYPE 4—BELONGING

The Romantic

You perceive life through a lens of melancholy and fantasy, amplifying its beauty and its tragedy alike. There's a poetic dance in your heart, and you're always in search of the right rhythm that resonates with the depth of your feelings.

Every moment is an opportunity to paint a picture more vivid, more intense. You transform mundane experiences into memorable encounters. A casual chat isn't just a conversation—it's an exchange of hearts. A mere glance becomes a silent sonnet, a whispered promise of something more.

But in your quest to see a world steeped in romantic hues, there's a risk of distancing yourself from reality and feeling estranged when the world doesn't match your vivid dreams.

MEET MS. SOPHIA, WHO WOVE MAGICAL TALES

> At my daughter, Oli's, Waldorf preschool, Ms. Sophia was the quintessential Romantic Artist. Every day, she crafted enchanting stories, making seasons, trees, and clouds feel alive. With her, the mundane became truly magical, filling each day with wonder.
>
> I vividly recall a parent-teacher meeting with her. Instead of just reporting on my daughter's progress, Sophia painted a poetic picture. She described Oli's imaginative playtime tales, her compassionate reaction to a fallen bird, and her spirited description of rain.
>
> Sophia's gift? Seeing the deep emotions and beauty in ordinary moments.
>
> But it was more than her romantic view of daily life that

TYPE 4—BELONGING

identified her as a Type 4. When she voiced concerns about reaching every child, her emotional intensity was palpable.

This was a teacher who deeply loved her students. With Ms. Sophia, there was an ever-present tide of emotions, making the everyday feel deeply meaningful.

These nicknames contain layers of meaning. Let's dive into the traits of and unravel the complexities of this romantic archetype.

PERSONALITY TRAITS OF TYPE 4

Desire: To Feel Seen and Loved

At your core, you crave love and recognition for your authentic self. You often feel unique and overlooked, harboring the belief that your distinctiveness will draw the affection you seek. This creates a paradox within you, as you believe your uniqueness is both the barrier to love and the key to attaining it. Artistic expression becomes your way to showcase your unique charm and value.

You crave profound emotional connections, but they always feel just out of reach—never aligning with your ideal fantasy. Your path to fulfillment lies in understanding that genuine appreciation isn't about being perceived perfectly or with utmost intensity. It's about feeling connection in all expressions—even the most common, mundane ones.

Emotion: Grief and Melancholy (Internalized Sadness)

You are drawn to sadness, like a magnet, pulling it into your heart. This sadness evolves into a melancholy and longing that colors your demeanor.

While your melancholy seems to validate your authenticity, there's a tendency to dramatize sadness more than truly feel it. Instead of connecting with its genuine essence, you embellish it, making the

TYPE 4—BELONGING

world's sorrow feel distinctively yours. This perpetual sense of longing—always wanting what seems just out of reach—becomes a constant in your life.

Fixation: Envy

Your mind crafts vibrant scenes, illustrating what others might possess and what you seem to lack. This sentiment stokes your rich imagination, serving as both a gift and a challenge.

You fixate on what you perceive to be missing in your life—usually connection. You often imagine others as having more or feeling deeper connections than reality suggests. This cycle of grief, longing, and envy erodes your self-love and stands in the way of wholeheartedly accepting your distinct path.

Shadow: Resentment

Resentment is the sting you feel when you sense you're overlooked or misunderstood. It's easy for you to harbor feelings of bitterness towards those who appear to sail smoothly or gain more attention.

This shadow side can push you to retreat, isolate. Deep within, you cling to old hurts and sabotage promising relationships and chances—expecting others to let you down in the end. Recognizing and working through this shadow can help you cultivate healthier relationships, truly embrace your unique journey, and find contentment in your heart.

MEET SUE, WHO JOURNEYED FROM RESENTMENT TO RECOGNITION

> My client Sue is a classic example of an Enneagram Type 4 wrestling with resentment. At work, she often feels like she's on the sidelines, overshadowed by her peers. She craves acknowledgement for the unique spin she brings to the table.

TYPE 4—BELONGING

Yet, every time someone else gets the spotlight or seems to climb the ladder with ease, it stings.

Together, Sue and I are using the Enneagram of Essence as our compass. Our aim? To steer her away from those waves of envy and toward the warm shores of self-nurturance. Through this process, she's beginning to feel a deeper connection to herself—a belonging that isn't dependent on external recognition.

Here's where the magic is happening. As Sue's focus has shifted towards her essence and an inner sense of belonging, something remarkable is unfolding. Her growing inner nourishment is cultivating an external environment where recognition flows more naturally. Her unique contributions are now receiving more attention and appreciation than ever.

She has become an example of inclusiveness—fostering an environment of belonging and intimacy around her.

Sue's transformation serves as a inspiration for the Type 4 in each of us. But what does Type 4 actually feel like from within? Let's dive into the experiences of this type in your body, exploring the sensations of both its personality and essence.

SOMATIC EXPERIENCE OF TYPE 4

Energetic Direction: Inward

Compared to the other directions of your heart—the Type 2's outward focus or the Type 3's balancing act—your Type 4 turns inward, delving into your deep emotional landscape. Your heart is like an ocean of complex emotions, where you dive deeper and deeper searching for your true individuality.

TYPE 4—BELONGING

For instance, in a social settings where everyone is wearing similar outfits, you defy the norm. You will wear something distinctively different, reflecting your unique style and feelings. Your internal compass consistently guides you towards what feels deeply authentic, influencing your decisions based on inner resonance rather than external expectations.

In Stress: Individualistic

To the outside world, you give off an air of mystery. Internally, your emotional landscape is an intense sea—always churning, always deeply felt. Your breath is heavy, fueled by a sense of longing and incompleteness. Your chest holds a deep ache—the weight of envy or melancholy for what seems missing.

Your eyes are vibrant yet tinged with nostalgia and flickering with jealousy—windows into your deep, complex inner world. A deep desire beats in your heart, searching for an even more authentic identity, yearning to be valued for your unique self.

With Essence: Embodied Belonging

As you tap into your essence, a beautiful undercurrent flows through you, soothing the stormy seas of your emotions. Within, a wellspring of love radiates, like a song humming just for you. Every note wraps you in warmth, creating a deep bond with yourself and the world around.

Your hands relax, often resting over your heart or lying open in your lap, signaling an openness to both giving and receiving love.

Your breath deepens, filling your lungs and nourishing your cells. The heaviness in your heart begins to dissolve, replaced by a gentle warmth. Your eyes soften, reflecting the essence of inner beauty.

Take a moment to fully immerse yourself in this loving presence, as it guides you towards embracing the mature, balanced Type 4 you're evolving into.

TYPE 4—BELONGING

MATURE TYPE 4 — FIXATION TO ESSENCE

Growth as a Type 4 revolves around embracing the inherent beauty and belonging that lies within your heart. It's about cherishing your unique essence while also valuing your shared humanity.

Imagine yourself as an ancient ocean—once you were a restless tide, ever-shifting and yearning, now you are a deep, serene sea, gracefully embracing your waves. In this version of yourself belonging doesn't arise from external validation or transient connections. Rather, it is an inner radiance that embraces you, regardless of life's fluctuations.

Remember that familiar feeling of being an outsider?

It's maturing into a glow of inner intimacy. You now radiate a sense of belonging that you've nurtured from within. Instead of dwelling on the past or daydreaming of the future, you're fully present, savoring each moment with the affirmation that you belong just as you are.

And, what about your old feelings of envy?

They've been replaced by the light of true authenticity, guiding you to the kind of beauty you've always yearned for. Your sense of individuality has matured. Once a cause for inner turmoil, it now serves as an inspiration to those around you. Your sense of belonging is infectious, touching everyone in your orbit.

While you've matured, your uniqueness remains. You bring creativity to each moment, and through this individual expression, you inspire others toward self-discovery and inner belonging. It's the intimate dance of your uniqueness intertwined with shared humanity that makes you truly whole.

Isn't it a profound process of self-discovery and love?

As we draw this chapter to a close, I'd like to share more of my Type 4 facet. Remember my story of nostalgic longing for the past? Now, I'll share the steps I took to find genuine belonging in the present.

I HAVE AN INVISIBLE CORD THAT STRETCHES MILES BACK INTO MY PAST

In my mid-thirties, I moved to the Western North Carolina mountains, a picturesque landscape that is worlds apart from my hometown in North Central Florida. Since then, I have found myself persistently being swept away by a soft undercurrent of longing.

This longing isn't for the hot, humid climate of Florida or for the flat, sandy landscapes that contrast the majestic Blue Ridge Mountains I now call home. In fact, I relish the fresh mountain air, the romantic smell of sweetgrass, and the serenity that stands in stark comparison to Florida's energy. However, a part of me remains tethered to my hometown like an invisible cord that stretches miles back to my past.

It's the Type 4 within me, resonating like a broken record replaying nostalgic memories of my hometown—the familiar streets, the comforting rhythm.

It projects fantasies about my past, stirring an illusion that seems preferable to the reality I live in. Working with the essence of Type 4 has shown me that my yearning for my hometown is less about the physical location and more about a certain sense of intimacy and belonging it symbolizes.

This yearning embodies the Type 4's need for connection and intimacy, a longing that manifests itself through an idealized version of reality. This yearning for true belonging has found a symbol in my old hometown. I know that this longing isn't meant to be satisfied by external sources. It's not about relocating or recreating Florida in the mountains.

TYPE 4—BELONGING

It's about recognizing that this deep yearning for connection and intimacy, is an inward journey.

Now, when nostalgia sweeps through me, I cherish my memories but work to remember the inner home within. I honor my past without allowing it to overshadow the beautiful moments with my children, the excitement of the seasons, or our community's sense of togetherness.

Through this self-connection, I unearth a home no physical location could provide, a sense of belonging that transcends geographical boundaries—an intimacy with no conditions.

Thank you for accompanying me on this intimate journey. I hope my stories and insights have ignited deeper introspection within you.

Next, you'll find practical steps for embodying your Type 4 essence, designed to help you move beyond limiting personality traits and integrate this wisdom into your daily life. These resources are an *introduction* to the embodiment path — setting the stage for deeper explorations available in my full programs.

For a FREE printable copy of this embodiment guide for all 9 types, please visit my website: EnneagramofEssence.com

EMBODIMENT
PATH TO BELONGING
EMBRACING TYPE 4 ESSENCE

JOURNEY INTO ESSENCE
The Enneagram of Essence's practical power is rooted in embodying essence and releasing limiting patterns. This brief guide to embodying Type 4's belonging is my gift, setting the stage for a much deeper exploration available in my full programs.

CONNECTION THROUGH TYPE 4 ESSENCE
Even though Type 4 is not my primary type, its essence fills me with a deep sense of inner belonging and connection. It invites authenticity and depth in my interactions with the world. *How could Type 4 essence enrich your inner and outer world?*

NATURE'S BEAUTY
Consider the profound beauty and resonance you feel in the presence of the ocean. This mirrors the rich spirit of Type 4, where beauty and belonging weave through the fabric of life.

MIND-BODY WELLNESS
Research indicates that embracing inner experiences of beauty and connection can relieve anxiety and stress, encouraging a deep sense of belonging within.

© 2023 Enneagram of Essence. All rights reserved.

TYPE 4—BELONGING

EMBODIMENT
PATH TO BELONGING
EMBRACING TYPE 4 ESSENCE

STEP 1: IDENTIFY PORTALS TO BELONGING

Identify what ignites feelings of inner belonging for you — nature, memories, loving people, etc. For me, visualizing the ocean's depth evokes a profound sense of intimate resonance within.

What symbols or experiences spark inner connection for you?

Incorporate elements like colors, textures, flavors, scents and sounds that mirror this quality into your space, as reminders of your Type 4 journey.

STEP 2: FEEL AND ANCHOR BELONGING

Notice the distinct way beauty and belonging feel within you. When I tap into this essence, I feel a sense of returning home — like I am deeply woven within the "fabric" of life.

What does inner radiance feel like in your body?

Practice feeling and anchoring this essence deeply throughout your nervous system — visualize and feel it flow through you, influencing your posture, movements, and perceptions.

© 2023 Enneagram of Essence. All rights reserved.

Embodiment
Path to Belonging
Embracing Type 4 Essence

Step 3: Center Belonging

Make an effort to notice and value the essence of inner beauty and belonging in people around you. Focus on essence when noticing someone's personality.

Think about how centering essence could change your understanding and appreciation of people with the primary Type 4.

How could this practice deepen your understanding and connections with people primarily identified as Type 4?

Step 4: Create a Practice

Incorporate these steps into a flexible and creative practice, bringing it into your daily routine from a week to a month. Focus on portals that ignite belonging and connection. Through regular engagement, embodying true beauty will become more and more effortless.

How will integrating these practices transform your daily life?

© 2023 Enneagram of Essence. All rights reserved

Embodiment
Path to Belonging
embracing type 4 essence

Step 5: Abstain from Limiting Traits

Make space within yourself to cultivate belonging. Type 4 personality traits serve as survival mechanisms so it's important to release them gently, leaning on inner resources for support.

Mindfully identify and release Type 4 patterns that detract from your essence, including:

Excessive Emotional Introspection
Shift your focus from inward emotions to appreciating the simplicity of your surroundings.

Dwelling on the Past
Release nostalgia by anchoring a present sense of belonging within every part of you.

Guarding Inner Resources
Share your knowledge and wisdom. Recognize that your inner resources are abundant.

Pressured Pursuit of External Validation
Cultivate a sense of inner worth and belonging, independent of external approval.

Comparison and Envy
Redirect thoughts of comparison to feelings of inner belonging — use comforting rituals.

© 2023 Enneagram of Essence. All rights reserved.

TYPE 4—BELONGING

EMBODIMENT
PATH TO BELONGING
EMBRACING TYPE 4 ESSENCE

STEP 5: ABSTAIN FROM LIMITING TRAITS
Mindfully identify and release Type 4 patterns that detract from your essence, including:

IDENTITY IN SUFFERING
Recognize the range of your authenticity, allowing yourself to feel cared for beyond your struggles.

ROMANTICIZING EMOTIONAL PAIN
Practice allowing emotions *move* through you without clinging to the pain.

INDULGING IN SELF-PITY
Focus on inner connection and empowerment instead of feelings of victimhood.

CLINGING TO UNIQUENESS
Celebrate common humanity and shared emotions — authenticity in yourself and others.

AVOIDING THE ORDINARY
Discover beauty in the everyday, creating spaces that remind you of life's *simple* beauty.

YEARNING FOR WHAT'S MISSING
Center the beauty and connection in what is present.

© 2023 Enneagram of Essence. All rights reserved.

TYPE 4—BELONGING

EMBODIMENT
Path to Belonging
EMBRACING TYPE 4 ESSENCE

Step 5: Abstain from Limiting Traits
Mindfully identify and release Type 4 patterns that detract from your essence, including:

Idealized Fantasies
Balance daydreaming with practices that foster inner belonging and beauty.

Fear of Insignificance
Affirm your intrinsic worth — ground in the inclusiveness of the natural world.

Sense of Defectiveness
Embrace imperfections as your authentic path.

Avoidance of Mundane Tasks
See routine tasks as opportunities for deeper connection with life's rich full tapestry

---

Use Step 5 as a bridge, not fixed rules. By centering essence, your personality traits will naturally relax into the nourishing qualities of inner beauty and belonging.

Let's conclude with a moment of integration through this guided meditation—opening the door to inner connection.

© 2023 Enneagram of Essence. All rights reserved.

GUIDED MEDITATION FOR TYPE 4

I encourage you to find a comfortable position, relax your body, and gently soften your focus. Read this slowly and with ease, twice—first to visualize the imagery, and then again to deeply connect with the sensations it evokes.

Relax your eyes.
Take a slow, deep breath.

You're at the edge
of a vast ocean.

Feel the soft sand
cushioning your feet.

A warm breeze
caresses your face.

Around you,
the salty essence
of the sea.

Beyond,
the ocean beckons,
inviting you to its depth.

Above,
the sky leans in,
embracing the horizon.

TYPE 4—BELONGING

GUIDED MEDITATION FOR TYPE 4

*Feel the ocean
deep in your heart.*

*It is profound,
intimate.*

*Watch . . .
Waves come closer.
See their rhythmic dance.*

*Listen . . .
The ocean sings.
A melody of depth and radiance.*

*Like the ocean,
you embrace.
You belong.*

*Like the ocean,
you are deep.
Beautiful.*

*The horizon merges,
blue deepens into deeper blue.*

*Find intimacy
in every ripple,
in every depth.*

GUIDED MEDITATION FOR TYPE 4

Sense a deep connection within.
A profound inner belonging.

Pause for a moment.

How did that meditation feel? Could you sense the intimacy and deep belonging of the ocean?

If that meditation resonated, it's because you accessed the spirit of belonging, which is not confined to external forms of life. The ocean's depth acts as a portal, yet true belonging is an internal, intrinsic part of you.

This is your journey. Absorb these suggestions at your pace—let them take root. When you're ready, turn the page and join me in discovering the essence of Type 3. Let's embrace your facets of achievement, productivity, and true value.

TYPE 3—VALUE

WORTH & WHOLENESS

KEY ELEMENTS

- **Center**—Heart, Love, & Sadness
- **Direction**—Balanced Focus
- **Personality**—Productive Achiever
- **Essence**—Value, Wholeness, Inner Worth

Do you ever find yourself...

- Driven to achieve in a way that overshadows all other aspects in your life?
- Compelled to project a picture-perfect image of success?
- Staying productive to avoid vulnerability?

There is a facet of your personality that moves with the ambitious nature of Type 3. And even deeper, your inner essence shines with inherent value.

TYPE 3—VALUE

Have you ever felt...

- Spontaneous awe when gazing at a sunset?
- The inherent value of simply being alive?
- That life itself is effortlessly impressive?

To some degree, each of us resonates with the impressive nature of Type 3—a heart that seeks genuine value and intrinsic worth. We all need to feel whole and complete in this world with never-ending projects. The essence of this type is a portal to inherent worth, a natural value and wholeness embedded in the simplest moments of life

Consider this a call to stop chasing value through achievement, productivity, and an impressive image.

Instead, cultivate an inner sense of value that can still be felt in the moments of simplicity and rest. By embracing this essence, you become an example of inherent worth, inspiration, and admiration in a world swayed by superficial competition. Let me tell you about the part of me that resonates with Type 3.

THAT PART OF ME THAT SEEKS PRAISE

> This type doesn't take the lead in my persona, but it has played a key role many times. Whether Type 3 spotlights as your primary type or just plays a supporting role, I hope my story sparks your own.
>
> Within me, Type 3 manifests as a challenge to feel value in my authentic path—particularly when it doesn't garner external recognition. This became glaringly clear during my initial job in my profession, where I faced the temptation to prioritize accolades over staying true to myself.

TYPE 3—VALUE

Fresh out of graduate school, fueled by my Type 3 traits of seeking recognition and success, I accepted a job at the US Department of Veterans Affairs. The praise and validation from my family and the advice to wear a suit pushed me further onto an inauthentic path.

Do you recall a time when you made a life decision for societal praise and recognition, veering you away from your authentic self?

I deviated from my passion for therapy and found myself coordinating programs—distanced from direct client care. The "suit" I wore for eight long years became a symbol, not of prestige, but of me drifting from my authentic self.

Yet, the arrival of motherhood was more than just a new chapter—it marked a seismic shift, a transformation I'll unravel later in this chapter. Suffice to say, its profound influence spurred a deep searching for my authentic meaning.

Though I still occasionally grapple with feelings of inadequacy and the urge to seek outside approval, I've learned to access and cherish my intrinsic value, choosing authenticity over society's benchmarks of success.

I'll share more about my invaluable journey with Type 3 at the end of this chapter. For now, let's immerse in the vibrant world of this personality and its nourishing essence.

Take a moment.
Find your heart.
Prepare to be inspired.

WELCOME TO TRUE VALUE

I invite you to begin by looking for the essence of Type 3 within your own heart. Initially, this may be subtle and easy to overlook—yet it's as awe-inspiring as a radiant sunrise over a majestic mountain range. You'll find it in the simplicity of your heart and in life's everyday moments, offering a profound sense of meaning.

It's like having a cosmic cheerleader living within you—an uplifting presence who sees the light of inspiration woven into every moment of life.

Imagine your worth isn't something you earn from achievements or applause. Instead, think of it as a real feeling that comes from deep inside you, always there, like a nourishing background hum that assures, "I am enough as I am."

It's an inspiring part of you, don't you think?

You were born with an intrinsic sense of worth, like the natural luster of a gemstone. However, life's struggles and societal expectations cast a shadow over your radiant essence. Your Type 3 traits shifted into survival mode, compelling you to vie for external accolades and achievements.

This led you to become driven and competitive, always in pursuit of success and recognition from the world outside yourself—desperately trying to reclaim your inherent worth.

Now, the Enneagram can help you elevate out of survival mode and towards a fundamental sense of value. Discover a self-worth that is rooted in a source much more resilient, palpable, and authentic than society's marks of success.

Imagine waking up each day feeling inherently valuable, just as you are. Where your sense of worth isn't tied to your to-do list or achievements, but simply exists within you.

TYPE 3—VALUE

This journey is about uncoupling your sense of self-worth from external praise and any behavioral marker of success and reconnecting to your inner value. Let's unpack the fundamental relationship between the essence of Type 3 and its personality traits.

TYPE 3'S QUEST FOR VALUE

Your Type 3 personality traits emerged from stress, pulling your attention away from your essence and into a fixation on accomplishments and external validation. You've been seeking value and worth through achieving goals and garnering praise.

This quest keeps you in a perpetual cycle of striving and achievement, obscuring the inner wholeness that already exists within you.

Consider my journey at the Veterans Administration. My Type 3 desire for external approval led me astray from my authentic path. I was too focused on meeting other people's expectations, which in turn delayed my dream of becoming a therapist. The praise I received felt empty because it wasn't aligned with my inner values.

Have there been times when your desire for approval overshadowed the value of your authentic path?

Here's a powerful insight—each trait of the "Overachiever" is a reflection of its essence. Your drive for excellence is an echo of the inner value residing deep within you. Your chase for success and recognition points to a deeper longing for true wholeness.

As we unpack each of these traits, consider them as hints pointing towards a universal essence of intrinsic value and completeness. Be curious about how these traits may be seeking their deeper, nourishing essence.

Take a moment to ponder these questions:

1. Do you ever chase goals at the expense of your well-being?
2. Do you crave achievement and accolades? Why?

3. Do you ever feel like you're wearing a mask to impress others?
4. When you don't reach a goal, do you doubt your worth?
5. Where do you find value—in accomplishments or in simply being alive?
6. When did you last feel truly worthy? Was it sparked by something outside or within you?

Allow these questions to linger and return to explore them more fully. Now, let's turn the pages back to your early childhood, visiting the origins of your Type 3 tendencies.

CHILDHOOD OF TYPE 3 — ESSENCE TO FIXATION

Thinking back to childhood, through the lens of Type 3. Do you remember how much importance was given to achievement? How much did it seem to matter when you brought home As, scored a goal, or earned a spot in the school play?

For the Type 3 in you, these moments defined your self-worth. Your value was measured more by your accomplishments than by your true self. This emphasis gradually distanced you from your sense of inner worth.

Sure, you excelled naturally, but under that discipline was a profound yearning for applause and praise.

Think about your parents. Unaware of how to see your true essence, they inadvertently linked your worth to your milestones and achievements. Was one parent particularly proud when you excelled in sports? Did another parent light up when you were on stage? These subtle cues shaped your growing sense of identity.

Driven by this need for approval, you started to adapt your behavior to align with the values that earned you praise. Over time, this flexibility morphed into a highly developed skill—a knack for swiftly adapting to what others value in you.

TYPE 3—VALUE

This is how the achiever in you formed. This pattern continued into your adult life, earning you various nicknames along the way. Let's explore them.

TYPE 3 NICKNAMES

The Achiever

From early on, you developed a strong drive for success, fueled by a desire for recognition and praise. You are adept at setting goals and tirelessly pursuing them, guided by your culture's metrics of success. You exceed expectations in multiple arenas—be it work, social circles, or family.

But, the quest goes deeper than surface-level accolades. Underneath, there's a search for meaning and value, a need to demonstrate your worth to both yourself and the world around you.

The Chameleon

It's a name you've earned through your ability to adapt and shape-shift, matching the "color" of your environment, aligning your image and behaviors with the expectations and values of those around you.

You are a master at social dynamics, proficient at reading rooms, deciphering what's valued, and tailoring your persona accordingly. But beneath this adaptable exterior, there's a deep-seated yearning to recognize and honor your inherent worth, independent of the roles you play.

Like a chameleon shifting hues, your external colors may change, but the essence of who you are remains innately impressive and valuable, regardless of the shade you portray.

The Producer

This title captures your ability to "turn it on" when needed—to step into the spotlight and deliver a captivating performance. Your charisma and adaptability allow you to shine in any role, attuned to what others expect.

And your productivity, it's almost superhuman—you produce far more than most, a testament to your driven nature. But beneath these dazzling performances there's a deeper longing, a wish for your performance to be more than a show, but a true expression of your authenticity.

MEET KYLE, WHO TURNED MARKETING INTO AN ART FORM

> My inspiring friend Kyle has a knack for taking the lemons life hands him, and instead of just making lemonade, he builds an entire lemonade empire. This is a man who's turned personal setbacks into powerful stories that add depth and authenticity to his brand. Whether it's a business failure or a personal crisis, Kyle has a unique way of turning obstacles into fuel for his next big idea.
>
> Classic to Type 3, Kyle's a big-picture person, always eyeing projects with heart and ambition.
>
> He's not one to get bogged down in the minute details. Instead, he focuses on the overarching vision, setting clear goals and striving towards them with relentless drive. He doesn't deal directly with the people his work impacts. Instead, he's the wizard behind the curtain, empowering others to step into the spotlight.
>
> One of Kyle's favorite projects involves taking life coaches

TYPE 3—VALUE

under his wing and teaching them how to harness the power of their own vulnerabilities.

He's a master at connecting with these aspiring coaches, understanding their dreams and fears, and showing them how to weave their own experiences into their personal brand. By helping them open up and share their authentic selves, he creates connections that draw clients in. And it's not just about business for Kyle—he genuinely cares about their success and growth.

Kyle's approach is a perfect example of a Type 3's capacity for achievement, adaptability, and production. He can switch gears at a moment's notice, always ready to seize the next opportunity that aligns with his goals and values. His journey goes to show that the power of a good story, combined with a little Type 3 ingenuity, can turn trials into opportunities for success.

These qualities aren't just nicknames or stereotypes—they're filled with traits that define Kyle's core personality. Let's unpack the most significant of these.

PERSONALITY TRAITS OF TYPE 3

Desire: To Feel Valuable, Successful, and Admired

Your core desire is to be admired. You want to stand out, to be impressive. Your achievements bring you brief satisfaction, a moment to relax and connect with a sense of value.

However, this fulfillment is temporary. It seems tied to your accomplishments, so you stay on an endless chase for the next achievement. Your image plays a critical role, serving as a daily reminder of your worth and fueling your ambition.

TYPE 3—VALUE

You use all aspects of life to bolster this image—friendships, career, education, possessions, relationships. Yet, any missed promotion or failure can feel devastating. It reveals an inner layer that feels valueless and deeply worthless, driving you to strive even harder to maintain your image.

Emotion: Deceit (Avoided Sadness)

Beneath the confidence you display lies a complex tapestry of emotions, including shame, sadness, and grief. Deceit, in this context, acts as your guard, shielding you from these deeper feelings. It's akin to a facade you maintain, rooted in the belief that your worth is solely defined by your achievements.

This deceit prevents you from confronting the genuine emotions beneath. You may worry that acknowledging these feelings could hinder your success or overwhelm you. However, as you gradually uncover and face these hidden layers, you'll find a truer version of yourself—one who engages with others meaningfully, independent of external accolades or validation.

Fixation: Vanity and Success

Your primary fixation is on the vanity of success. This doesn't mean you're vain in the conventional sense—it refers to your intense focus on creating an image of success and achievement. This fixation causes you to prioritize tasks that garner recognition over less visible yet vital tasks.

Failures or weaknesses are reframed and repressed to maintain your cultivated image. While avoiding situations of failure might seem impossible, you possess the ability to avoid truly *experiencing* them. You make failures stepping stones to success by highlighting the positive opportunities they bring.

Shadow: Inherent Unworthiness

Your primary shadow stems from a fear that, at the core, you lack inherent value or worth. As a child, you embodied intrinsic value, but this sense of worth became clouded as you encountered societal expectations and judgements.

This disconnect from your innate value fuels an underlying fear of being an imposter. You find yourself in a perpetual cycle, accumulating achievements to outrun your sense of unworthiness, often sacrificing your well-being, relationships, and true self-expression in the process.

Meet Susanna, Who Transitioned from Trophies to Tenderness

> I will always remember my dear client Susanna, not just because of her warm heart but because of the transformation that unfolded right before my eyes. She walked into my office, a recently retired medical provider, carrying herself with a confident crispness that hinted at her successful career.
>
> Yet her eyes told a different story. They were the eyes of someone who had swapped career accolades for wine bottles, trying to fill the void that her busy work life had once occupied.
>
> Slowing down was new terrain for Susanna, like a seasoned traveler suddenly finding herself in a foreign land without a map. Suddenly, she found herself shedding quiet tears, an unfamiliar experience that annoyed her, to say the least. Yet, behind her frustration, there was curiosity, recognition, and even a glimpse of hope.
>
> She recognized there was wisdom in this new phase of her life, a wisdom she was both eager and hesitant to explore.
>
> As our therapy progressed, we started diving into the depths of Susanna's heart, exploring the rich essence of her Type 3 personality—universal value, wholeness, and centered love. This wasn't just an exploration—it was an emotional journey, filled with twists and turns, but one that Susanna learned to trust, embrace, and even celebrate.

After about a year, a new Susanna unfolded, as if a beautiful butterfly had emerged from a cocoon. From a woman who once side-stepped vulnerability and focused on efficiency, she transformed into a tender, loving individual.

Surprisingly, what she once deemed her biggest weakness—emotional empathy and tenderness—became her strength and gift to others.

Susanna's journey shines as a light for the Type 3 in all of us. But what does Type 3 actually feel like from within? Let's dive into the sensations and experiences of this type in your body, exploring the intricacies of both its personality and essence.

SOMATIC EXPERIENCE OF TYPE 3

Energetic Direction: Balanced

Compared to the other directions of your heart—the Type 2's outward focus or the Type 4's inward focus—your Type 3 strikes a balance. You want your image and inner expression to align with what's considered valuable and successful in your chosen group or culture.

For instance, in an artistic group that values originality, you might wear bold, unique clothing and show a creative expression in your interactions. Conversely, in a corporate environment that values professionalism, you'd likely choose conservative, formal wear and behave in a focused, efficient manner to align with the expectations of success in that setting.

In Stress: Overachieving

On the outside, you are the picture of efficiency and poise. Yet, within, a constant striving churns—your pulse beats for your checklist of

TYPE 3—VALUE

ambitions and goals. There's a persistent tightness in your chest—carrying the burden of your drive for excellence. Each step is measured, deliberate—the rhythm of a mind marching towards victory.

Your eyes reflect a polished assurance, your smile a beacon of victory, yet beneath is a tireless quest for validation. Beyond the accomplishments you showcase, there lies a deeper longing—not merely to stand out, but to be genuinely valued.

With Essence: Embodied Value

Inside, a comforting warmth envelops you, like the gentle embrace of the morning sun. Life transcends accolades now—it's rooted in deep contentment. Your chest expands with a sensation that whispers, "I am enough." Each heartbeat carries pure self-worth, untied to achievements. A genuine sense of pride surrounds you, not for what you've done, but for simply being who you are.

Let this sensation permeate your being as we delve into our final section and get to know this type of maturity.

MATURE TYPE 3 — FIXATION TO ESSENCE

The key to Type 3 maturity is in recognizing your true value prior to achieving. Inherent worthiness is all-inclusive—it embraces moments of achievement and times of rest with equal pride.

Visualize yourself as the sun rising over the horizon, reveling in natural wholeness, regardless of the achievements the day will bring. In this version of yourself, value doesn't stem from external validation or transient accomplishments. Rather, it is an inner wholeness that embraces you, unaffected by life's fluctuations.

Remember your relentless drive for success?

It's settled into a grounded presence within you. The frantic pursuit of external validation has given way to a serene acceptance, a realization of your intrinsic worth. The quest for accolades has shifted into a celebration of your authentic path—a metamorphosis from seeking validation to embodying it.

Your outlook on the future has shifted too.

Gone are the days of striving to outperform yourself. Instead, you're rooted in the present, nourished by the meaning inherent in every moment of life. You've released the need to impress and have become an example of authenticity, embracing life in all its phases.

And your charisma has matured, too. Once used to seek admiration, it now serves to inspire and uplift others. The inner fulfillment you've nurtured doesn't just reside within you—it shines out, positively impacting those around you.

You're still you though—energetic, dynamic, and inspiring. It's your collective outlook that truly captures your maturity—recognizing your inherent value and uplifting others to see their own.

What an inspired journey, don't you think?

With that, I'm eager to conclude this chapter by revealing more about my own Type 3 journey—that time I wore a suit of inauthenticity and my path to finding inherent worth.

THE ATTENTION, THE RECOGNITION—IT FELT GOOD, ALMOST INTOXICATING

> "Congratulations," my family cheered when I announced the Veteran Administration internship. Their praise echoed in my ears like a sweet symphony. The attention, the recognition—it felt good, almost intoxicating. I even wore a suit to the interview, which felt more like a costume than a representation of my authentic self. But it didn't matter.

TYPE 3—VALUE

The Type 3 in me had set its eyes on the prize—a job that was impressive to everyone around me.

Over time, that suit became my second skin. The crisp lines of the pants and the stiff fabric did not represent me, but they mirrored the expectations others had of me. The advice I'd been given had not only influenced my wardrobe, but my entire trajectory at the Veterans Administration.

I was a therapist at heart, eager to connect with clients, delve into their journeys, and help them navigate their well-being.

I had always been fascinated by psychology and the Enneagram. I wanted to hone those skills, to apply them in a therapeutic setting. But my leadership saw something "impressive" in me—an ability to coordinate and lead. They encouraged me to walk an administrative path.

And so I did. I was drawn away from my authenticity by the allure of recognition. I found myself coordinating programs instead of engaging in the therapeutic work that fuels my spirit. When I attempted to carve out time for real talk-therapy with clients, I was steered back, reminded of my more "important" role within that system.

It was a jarring reflection of how far I had strayed from the journey my heart yearned to follow.

For eight long years, I remained on this superficial track. But when I got pregnant, everything changed. As my belly grew, so did my realization that I was living inauthentically. The Type 3 in me had been enticed by the external validation, but now I yearned for something more meaningful.

When my son arrived, I departed from the Veterans

Administration. It was liberating, despite the fear of becoming irrelevant or erasing my professional strides. I could not bear the idea of missing his early years for a job that had never truly resonated with my heart's calling. Thus, I welcomed motherhood, turning the act of being present with my child into my core practice.

My Type 3 tendencies still linger.

At times, I still face the sense of not accomplishing enough, or feeling inadequate. My small private practice and home-life with my children may not bring the external applause I once received, but they hold a significance that's far more profound and personally fulfilling.

The essence of Type 3 keeps me connected to authenticity. It's a practice I repeat, a source of inspiration that helps me to remember what truly matters—my children's laughter, the presence I bring to their world.

Thank you for accompanying me on this inspiring journey. I hope my stories and insights have ignited deeper introspection within you.

Next, you'll find practical steps for embodying your Type 3 essence, designed to help you move beyond limiting personality traits and integrate this wisdom into your daily life. These resources are an *introduction* to the embodiment path — setting the stage for deeper explorations available in my full programs.

For a FREE printable copy of this embodiment guide for all 9 types, please visit my website: EnneagramofEssence.com

TYPE 3—VALUE

Embodiment
Path to Value
embracing type 3 essence

Journey into Essence
The Enneagram of Essence's practical power is rooted in embodying essence and releasing limiting patterns. This brief guide to embodying Type 3's value is my gift, setting the stage for a much deeper exploration available in my full programs.

Value Through Type 3 Essence
Even though Type 3 is not my primary type, its essence adds inspiration and appreciation to my life, enhancing my sense of wholeness. *How could Type 3 essence enrich your inner and outer world?*

Nature's Impressiveness
Consider the natural awe inspired by watching a breathtaking sunrise. This simple, everyday marvel reflects the brilliance inherent in each new day. That's the valuable spirit of Type 3.

Mind-Body Wellness
Mind-body research shows that nurturing a sense of inner value can shift your stress responses, fostering deeper well-being and fulfillment beyond external accomplishments.

© 2023 Enneagram of Essence. All rights reserved.

EMBODIMENT
PATH TO VALUE
EMBRACING TYPE 3 ESSENCE

STEP 1: IDENTIFY PORTALS TO VALUE

Identify what ignites feelings of inner value and worth for you — nature, memories, inspiring people, etc. For me, imagining a child's quiet pride in their creation inspires natural value. There's no need for applause—awe is found in the act of creation itself.

What symbols or experiences spark inner value and wholeness for you?

Incorporate elements like colors, textures, flavors, scents and sounds that mirror this quality into your space, as reminders of your Type 3 journey.

STEP 2: FEEL AND ANCHOR VALUE

Notice the distinct way inner worth and natural wholeness feel within you. When I connect with this essence, I feel a brilliant warmth in my chest, filling my heart with bright inspiration and a pride that seems to be universal.

What does value feel like in your body?

Practice feeling and anchoring value deeply throughout your nervous system — visualize and feel it flow through you, influencing your posture, movements, and perceptions.

© 2023 Enneagram of Essence. All rights reserved.

TYPE 3—VALUE

Embodiment
Path to Value
embracing type 3 essence

Step 3: Center Value

Make an effort to notice and value the essence of worth and wholeness in people around you. Focus on essence when noticing someone's personality.

Think about how centering this essence could change your understanding and appreciation of people with the primary Type 3.

How could this practice deepen your understanding and connections with people primarily identified as Type 3?

Step 4: Create a Practice

Incorporate these steps into a flexible and creative practice, bringing it into your daily routine from a week to a month. Focus on portals that ignite awe, inspiration, and value. Through regular engagement, embodying inner value will become more and more effortless.

How will integrating these practices transform your daily life?

© 2023 Enneagram of Essence. All rights reserved.

EMBODIMENT
PATH TO VALUE
EMBRACING TYPE 3 ESSENCE

STEP 5: ABSTAIN FROM LIMITING TRAITS

Make space within yourself to cultivate true value. Type 3 personality traits serve as survival mechanisms so it's important to release them gently, leaning on inner resources for support.

Mindfully identify and release Type 3 patterns that detract from your essence, including:

PURSUIT OF VALIDATION
Shift focus from external approval to cultivating your inherent worth.

PURSUIT OF EXCELLENCE
Ease the drive for constant excellence by connecting with the warmth in your heart.

EMPHASIS ON IMAGE
Embrace your genuine self, use affirmations to celebrate your authenticity beyond any image.

OVERWORKING
Allow yourself to take breaks, integrating moments of yoga or mindfulness throughout your day to nurture balance and presence.

© 2023 Enneagram of Essence. All rights reserved.

EMBODIMENT
PATH TO VALUE
EMBRACING TYPE 3 ESSENCE

STEP 5: ABSTAIN FROM LIMITING TRAITS

Mindfully identify and release Type 3 patterns that detract from your essence, including:

COMPETITIVENESS
Redirect competitive urges towards collaborative growth. Cultivate a sense of value unrelated to external traits.

REPRESSION OF VULNERABILITY
Work to recognize and express your emotions. Make tenderness a tangible experience.

AVOIDANCE OF FAILURE
Normalize learning from mistakes by reflecting on them. Cultivate comfort in tenderness.

IMPERSONAL RELATIONSHIPS
Prioritize connection over surface-level interactions. Nurture depth with others.

SPEED AND EFFICIENCY
Take time to be present and mindful. Practice slow, deliberate movement — feel a sense of meaning within your body.

© 2023 Enneagram of Essence. All rights reserved.

EMBODIMENT
PATH TO VALUE
EMBRACING TYPE 3 ESSENCE

STEP 5: ABSTAIN FROM LIMITING TRAITS
Mindfully identify and release Type 3 patterns that detract from your essence, including:

SUPPRESSION OF DEPTH AND AUTHENTICITY
Embrace your emotions for a fuller life experience. Practice genuine self-expression.

HYPER-FOCUS ON GOALS
Devote at least as much time practicing mindfulness as setting goals.

FEAR OF MEDIOCRITY
Remember, your worth and value is independent from achievements and being exceptional,

---

Use Step 5 as a bridge, not fixed rules. By centering essence, your personality traits will naturally relax into the nourishing qualities of inner value, worth and wholeness.

Let's conclude with a moment of integration through this guided meditation—opening the door to inner value.

© 2023 Enneagram of Essence. All rights reserved.

TYPE 3—VALUE

GUIDED MEDITATION FOR TYPE 3

I encourage you to find a comfortable position, relax your body, and gently soften your focus. Read this slowly and with ease — first to visualize the imagery, and again to connect with the sensations it evokes.

Relax your eyes.
Take a deep breath in.

You're standing atop
a grand mountain.

Feel the solid ground
beneath your feet.

Cool morning breeze
touches your skin.

Inhale the scent
of tall pine trees
and fresh air.

Below,
a deep green expanse.

Above,
orange and pink herald the dawn.

Feel the sunrise
bright in your heart.

© 2023 Enneagram of Essence. All rights reserved.

GUIDED MEDITATION FOR TYPE 3

It's impressive,
radiant

Like this sunrise,
You were born to shine.

Watch...
The sun rises higher.
Warm rays touch everything.

Listen...
Life awakens.
A symphony begins.

Like the sun,
You share warmth.
You uplift.

Like the sun,
You spread light.
You inspire.

The sky transforms,
Colors paint its canvas.

Find value
In every hue,
every moment.

© 2023 Enneagram of Essence. All rights reserved.

GUIDED MEDITATION FOR TYPE 3

Sense a deeper wholeness.
A profound completeness.

You're not just watching the sunrise.
You are a part of it,
sharing its natural value.

Pause for a moment.

How did that meditation feel? Could you sense the natural impressiveness of the mountain sunrise?

If that meditation resonated, it's because you accessed the spirit of value, which is not confined to external forms of life. The sunrise acts as a portal, yet the essence of value and worth is an internal, intrinsic part of you.

This is your journey. Absorb these suggestions at your pace—let them take root. When you're ready, turn the page and join me in embracing yourself with Type 2. Let's discover your facets of self-love and compassion.

TYPE 2—COMPASSION

NURTURANCE & KINDNESS

KEY ELEMENTS

- **Center**—Heart, Love, & Sadness
- **Direction**—Outward Focus
- **Personality**—Selfless Giver
- **Essence**—Compassion, Kindness, Inner Nurturance

Do you ever find yourself...

- Compelled to help or support others, at your own expense?
- Wanting to be seen and appreciated as caring or selfless?
- Hurt when your kindness goes unnoticed or unacknowledged?

There is a facet of your personality that seeks love with the traits of a Type 2. And, even deeper, your essence resonates with its embracing nourishment.

TYPE 2—COMPASSION

Have you ever felt...

- A hug so deep that you seemed to merge with love itself?
- As if the universe itself was holding you in a warm embrace?
- Nourished by your own compassion, while giving to another?

Within every heart is the caregiving spirit of Type 2—a heart that longs for love and compassion. We all yearn for warmth and kindness in a world that often feels cold-hearted. The essence of this type is a portal to true compassion, kindness that embraces both others and yourself.

Consider this a call to stop chasing love and approval through giving.

Instead, anchor your worthiness within and discover that you are so much more than the care you provide. By embracing this essence you become an example of true kindness and inner nurturance in a world that has forgotten how to love itself and its neighbors. Let me tell you about the Type 2 part of me.

THAT PART OF ME THAT MARTYRS

> Though it's not my dominant type, I've grown to rely on this nurturing part of myself. Whether you relate to Type 2 occasionally or it represents your primary type—let my story inspire you to discover your own.
>
> The seeds of my Type 2 were lying dormant, waiting for the appropriate conditions to activate. And those conditions were motherhood. With the birth of my children, this latent archetype sprang forth like a wildfire spreading its tendrils throughout my relationships.

A relentless drive to fulfill everyone else's needs, except my own, eroded the early years of my family adventure.

In the thick of nurturing my children, balancing work, and shouldering household duties, my own needs faded to the background. This blind spot created a festering resentment, especially towards my husband, who was trying to find his own balance during this intense period.

Have you also placed the needs of others so high that your own well-being became dim, potentially breeding resentment?

For me, it took a raw moment in therapy to see the truth of this pattern. I realized, the root of my care-giving struggle wasn't my husband's fault—it was my own self-abandonment. It was time for another transformation.

When I recognized the Type 2 tendencies were at play, I turned to the essence of true compassion to guide my way. But the specifics of this transformation? That's a deeper dive I've reserved for the end of this chapter. Just know that this change didn't diminish my role as a mother—it enriched it.

First, let's get to know all the fascinating traits of this type and the nourishing essence at its heart.

Take a pause.
Feel your heart.
Prepare for a nurturing ride.

TYPE 2—COMPASSION

WELCOME TO TRUE COMPASSION

Let's begin this journey by tuning in to the nurturing essence of Type 2 that dwells within you. Radiating from your heart center is a kindness that's as soft and warm as the first light of a summer day. This quality shines with an abundance of love, nurturance, and caregiving.

It's like having an eternally loving mother within you, whose heart is so full it continually overflows.

Picture yourself in a state where compassion isn't merely a characteristic, but your intrinsic energy. True compassion isn't confined to your actions or how others treat you. It's a vibrant life-force that resonates effortlessly from within.

Now, this is a nourishing part of you, isn't it?

You entered this world immersed in universal love—like a tender sprout basking in the warm light of the sun. However, life's challenges cast a veil over this connection, dimming its warmth. Under stress, your Type 2 survival traits emerged—driving you to pursue true compassion through excessive giving.

This drove you into an unhealthy state of self-neglect and sacrifice, compulsively focusing on others' needs at your own expense—desperately trying to reconnect to universal love.

Here is where the Enneagram becomes your precious ally. It can nurture you out of survival mode and back to a natural state of love that emanates from a much deeper source than your actions or those of others.

Let's delve into the fundamental relationship between the essence of Type 2 and its personality traits.

TYPE 2'S QUEST FOR COMPASSION

Your Type 2 personality traits formed around childhood challenges and emotional scars, shifting your focus from inner essence to an external quest for love and validation. Your value, worth, and potential for love became entwined with pleasing and attending to others.

This quest entraps you in a tumultuous cycle of yearning for love and feeling profoundly disappointed, overshadowing your connection to the authentic love that is innately yours.

For example, the way I played out self-sacrifice as a new mother was the epitome of this pattern. I neglected my own needs to the point of exhaustion, believing it was for the greater good of my family. However, this self-neglect led to a cycle of resentment and disappointment. I harbored unspoken expectations that my husband would intuit my needs, and when he didn't, it deepened my resentment. It was a harsh realization that by not voicing my needs, I was obstructing my path to genuine self-care and a truly overflowing heart.

Have you ever been so absorbed in caring for others that you ignored your own needs, and then felt resentment when those around you didn't recognize your efforts?

Here's an Enneagram insight—every trait of the "Caregiver" aims to mirror its essence—universal compassion. Your seemingly selfless inclination to attend to the needs of others is an attempt to express the intrinsic love and care that is fundamental to life. Yet, when this care is directed outward to the exclusion of yourself, it is merely an imitation of its universal source.

Each characteristic of this personality type, when unpacked, reveals a quest for the profound essence of true compassion. As we explore each trait in the next sections, consider how they fundamentally relate to their essence.

Take a moment to ponder these questions:

TYPE 2—COMPASSION

1. Do you ever give to others at the expense of your own needs? Why?
2. Do you ever seek appreciation for your kindness and generosity? How?
3. Is there a part of you that feels unworthy if you're not helping someone?
4. Do you feel uncomfortable or less valuable when you're not helping?
5. How do you react when your efforts go unacknowledged? Does it upset you?
6. When did you last feel true compassion? Was it sparked by something outside or within you?

Allow these questions to resonate and revisit them for deeper reflection. Now, let's turn to the place where the Type 2 traits began to crystalize, your childhood.

CHILDHOOD OF TYPE 2 — ESSENCE TO FIXATION

Think back on your childhood, through the lens of Type 2.

You may notice that your world was a symphony of needs—your family's needs, your friends' needs, your community's needs, and even your teachers' needs. Yet, yours seemed to play second fiddle, if they were ever heard at all.

Do you remember your childhood home? Was it filled with sounds of life—laughter, arguments, whispered secrets, and hushed lullabies? You were there, amidst it all, a little beacon of love and care.

Without even realizing it, you were absorbing the unspoken rules—to be loved means to be helpful, to be valued means to be needed.

At school, you were the friend everyone could rely on. Your classmates knew they could count on you for help with their homework, a listening ear, or a comforting word. It felt good to be needed. Your heart was open to everyone—your compassion ever-flowing.

TYPE 2—COMPASSION

But what about you?

Who was there to hear your needs, to understand your desires, to support your dreams? In the process of caring for others, your own voice got lost. You learned that love was something to be earned through caregiving—through self-sacrifice.

Deep down, you yearned for a love that was unconditional, a love that included not just others, but yourself as well.

This is how your inner caregiver took form—compassion sprouted from a fundamental misreading of love. Seeking approval, you began tailoring your actions to reflect what seemed most appreciated. This strategy gradually evolved into a keen sensitivity to others' needs while sidelining your own.

It's time to transition from your childhood origins to the core traits of your adult personality, commonly distinguished by three nicknames.

TYPE 2 NICKNAMES

The Caregiver

You have an ability to care for others, that is both innate and conditioned. From a young age, you were a comforting presence, lending a hand or offering a kind word to those in distress. This inclination to prioritize others' needs, always eager to ease their burdens, has grown with you.

Rooted in a desire for true compassion and a longing to be loved, this trait has become an ingrained part of who you are. It shapes your interactions daily, whether you're supporting friends, standing by family, or showing empathy to colleagues.

Your consistent focus on others' well-being—when disconnected from essence—becomes a burden and leads to resentment.

TYPE 2—COMPASSION

The Helper

From an early age, you learned to connect your self-worth with being helpful—offering comfort, lending an ear, and providing support. Though you excel in responding to others' needs—it's sometimes your idea of their needs rather than their true needs.

Your eagerness stems from an intense drive to feel important in others' lives—to feel worthy of love. To this end, you stretch yourself thin and overcommit socially. Deep down, you long to spend time alone—for time to rejuvenate and to reclaim your energy for yourself.

The Nurturer

You are the embodiment of nurturance and caring, naturally expressing love and affection—secretly seeking it in return. Your nurturing nature lies in your essence, yet it's your nurturing efforts that become an obstacle. When you allow compassion to flow without effort, your inherent energy creates safe, comforting environments for others, both physically and emotionally.

Your kindness and empathy draw people to you as they seek solace and comfort. As you continue to be a haven for others, remember that it's equally essential to extend this same nurturing care to yourself—balancing your desire to care for others with self-compassion and love.

MEET CLARA, A LOVING NANNY WHO FORGOT TO LOVE HERSELF

> For some time, our family was graced by Clara, a nanny whose nurturing presence was felt by everyone. Her energy was like a comforting blanket, offering warmth and kindness. She lavished care and attention on my children, nurturing not only their bodies but also their spirits. And we all loved her sweet, whimsical nature.
>
> Yet, there was something else we noticed about Clara—a

TYPE 2—COMPASSION

shadow that lurked beneath her nurturing light. We noticed that she rarely took time to tend to her own needs.

She would shrug off her lunch breaks, instead devoting that time to the children. She'd speak proudly of sacrificing sleep to assist other "needy" mothers in our community. It may seem odd to boast to your employer about not being at your best. But through the Type 2 lens, we believe we will be valued for being a martyr. She seemed to expect appreciation for this trait.

Clara embodied the nurturer who forgot herself in the process. Her way, despite being filled with so much love for others, was marked by a neglect of her own needs. It was as if she was wearing her self-neglect like a subtle cry for recognition and appreciation that often went unheard.

These nicknames hold much detail. Let's go further and explore the traits that define the Selfless Caregiver.

PERSONALITY TRAITS OF TYPE 2

Desire: To Be Loved and Appreciated

All your Type 2 personality traits stem from a desire for love. During your childhood, moments of affection and appreciation were linked to the times you were helpful. This association created a deep-seated belief that love and appreciation are the rewards for your caretaking. As a result, you've developed a strong drive to be helpful and supportive, hoping your deeds will earn you the love and recognition you need.

You've woven indispensability into your identity, fearing you might be overlooked or even cast aside if not perpetually needed. This often leads to becoming everyone's go-to support, from solving problems to lending an ear. Unhealthily, this may slide into enabling, as you

TYPE 2—COMPASSION

subconsciously keep others dependent, fostering codependency where your value is tied to their reliance on you—a pattern that hinders both your well-being and their growth.

Emotion: Pride (Externalized Sadness)

Your sense of pride is deeply tied to your role as a caregiver. You validate your importance by silently tallying the help you've given, reassuring yourself with thoughts like, "They need me" and "They couldn't do this without me". This internal scorekeeping becomes a shaky foundation for your self-esteem—propped up by the continuous care you give, fueling your perception of being irreplaceable.

However, when the effort you pour into your caregiving is not met with the appreciation you need, feelings of rejection and disrespect surge, leading to resentment or even rage. Such intense emotions reveal the cycle at the core of your quest for genuine love and affection and significantly shape your emotional landscape.

Fixation: Flattery and Ingratiation

Your deep need for appreciation leads you to please others through charm and flattery, such as complimenting a friend's appearance each time you get together. It's a strategy to earn love and form bonds, but it may keep genuine connections at bay.

This habit may hinder the authentic relationships you seek. At times, your compliments or flattery, even if true to your opinion, may come more from an old habit than authentic expression in the moment. This tendency creates a subtle barrier in your relationships, because your charm may feel fueled by anxiety and neediness.

Shadow: Conditional Love

While you generously pour your heart and effort into helping, there's an underlying expectation of recognition and appreciation. Your generosity often comes with pure intentions, hoping to guide and uplift those you care for. But in moments of stress or vulnerability, expectations attach themselves to your well-meant care.

It's natural to feel hurt when you offer advice out of love, only to see it set aside by a friend. In moments when your gestures of support are not acknowledged, your love becomes overshadowed by a wave of hurt and resentment. This response may carry the weight of every unnoticed effort, every thankless task, and every time you feel undervalued.

Recognizing this pattern is a step toward understanding yourself more deeply. This reaction doesn't define you—it simply highlights the complex, often conditional layers within your expressions of care. Approach these feelings with kindness towards yourself, treat them as signposts pointing towards deeper self-love.

MEET JANE, A CAREGIVER WHO LEARNED SELF-CARE

> I once worked with a client, Jane, whose Type 2 traits were easy to spot. Whenever we interacted, she never missed a chance to shower me with praise and always seemed eager to ensure my comfort.
>
> While Jane wasn't a professional caregiver, everyone recognized her as a nurturer—she took care of everyone around her.
>
> It was both poignant and saddening to observe her navigate her own vulnerable moments while simultaneously checking in on my emotional state—anticipating and addressing my needs *as she imagined them*. A hallmark of Type 2 behavior—struggling to accept care and be supported. Even attempting to nurture her own therapist.
>
> Beneath Jane's charm, there was a deep well of unmet needs and feelings of emptiness. She was always helping others, but

TYPE 2—COMPASSION

she had this gnawing dissatisfaction and loneliness lingering under her smiley exterior. She was trying to fill a void with external appreciation while neglecting her own needs.

So, we began focusing on the Path of Nourishment. The goal was to tap into the essence of universal compassion. But first we had to help Jane understand that she was valuable beyond being caring and she deserved love regardless of how helpful she was.

Through dedicated essence practices Jane began to check in with herself more. She started acknowledging her feelings—and more importantly, her needs. We worked on setting boundaries also—helping her realize that it was okay to say no when she felt overwhelmed.

Over time, Jane's approach to giving matured. She found she could still be of service to others—but it no longer felt like a bid for appreciation. Instead, it was genuine, arising from her growing self-love and the essence of true compassion.

It was heartwarming for me to witness Jane's journey, highlighting how impactful this path can be. But what does Type 2 actually feel like from within? Let's dive into the sensations and experiences of this type in your body, exploring the intricacies of both its personality and essence.

SOMATIC EXPERIENCE OF TYPE 2

Energetic Direction: Outward

Compared to the other directions of your heart—the Type 4 that turns inward or the Type 3 that balances—your Type 2 orients outward, radiating your innate kindness and care to those around you. You actively seek opportunities to engage outwardly with compassion, kindness, and bonds of affection.

For instance, if a friend seems even slightly down, while others may be too busy to notice, your outward nature will drive you to notice and comfort them. Whether offering advice or just listening, you aim to provide comfort and a touch of kindness to lift their spirits.

In Stress: Over-giving

On the outside, your presence radiates care, like arms always open to embrace. Yet within, a vigilant sensitivity to others' emotions keeps you on constant alert. Your heart reaches out, flowing with gestures of comfort and support.

However, this well-intentioned giving carries an invisible weight, a silent yearning for your kindness to be acknowledged.

While you outwardly project cheerfulness, a tangible heaviness lingers in your chest—a somatic echo of your need for reciprocated care and validation. Each unacknowledged gesture pulls at your heart, a silent plea for the empathy you generously share to be returned.

With Essence: Embodied Compassion

As survival mode dissolves, a nurturing self-compassion emerges—like a soft exhale, you embrace yourself before extending to others. The once insistent drive to nurture eases, your breath deepens with tranquility. Your shoulders unburden, releasing the weight of the world. From this center of self-love, your kindness diffuses naturally, inwardly nourished before it cascades outward.

Feel the tender balance of both giving and receiving through your whole being—your nervous system anchored in true compassion. Savor this warm sensation as we venture into our last section and get to know the Type 2 in maturity.

TYPE 2—COMPASSION

MATURE TYPE 2 — FIXATION TO ESSENCE

The hallmark of your Type 2 maturation is transitioning from a need for external appreciation to discovering a deep source of love within. This self-compassion flourishes, generously extending to yourself and others unconditionally.

Imagine yourself as an evergreen—resilient and nourished, exuding warmth amidst the cold. In this nurtured state, you offer warmth and care, not just to others, but also to yourself, flourishing in all seasons of life.

Remember your relentless urge to care for others?

It has evolved. Now, a natural, overflowing love for others defines your interactions. The motivation behind your acts of love has shifted profoundly—they're now expressions of an abundant, universal compassion.

Your relationships have transformed as well. They've deepened, grown richer as you find the delicate balance between caring for others and honoring your own needs. Your connections are more genuine and reciprocal.

Past resentments and expectations fade as you become more aware of your own needs and how to care for yourself. Your care now radiates effortlessly, not anchored to specific actions but as an aura of nurturance. Your acts of kindness are now inspired by an unconditional, universal love that neither seeks acknowledgement nor requires self-sacrifice.

Caring for yourself, you become more attuned to the true meaning of love and support. You transform the role of a caregiver—you become a beacon of self-respect and self-love.

It's a gorgeous transformation, can you see it?

With that, I'd love to conclude this chapter with personal insights from my Type 2 path. Recall when I shared about my early motherhood, marked by constant caregiving and sacrifice? I'm happy to share that those overreaching sacrifices turned into stepping stones, helping me find a deeper love and acceptance for my own needs. Let me show you how it unfolded.

I POURED FROM A CUP THAT WAS NEVER REFILLED

Once upon a chaotic and beautiful chapter in my life, I was a mom to two tiny humans—their ages a mere two years apart. The days blurred together as I navigated my way through endless diaper changes, crying, laughing, and moments of quiet meaning.

I was relentless in my pursuit to be the *most* loving, kindest, and fully attached mother I could be. But, as I poured from a cup that I never refilled, my reserves depleted. My heart was heavy with unspoken frustrations, my body was tired and aching.

My husband was doing his best—navigating the challenges of a high-pressure job, carrying the weight of a provider. But amidst my feelings of being undervalued and my own unacknowledged needs, I found myself resenting his efforts to tend to his own well-being. At the heart of it, I envied his ability to care for himself.

I was unable to turn my attention inward, remember myself, or take responsibility for my own needs. Instead, I kept score of everything I was doing for the family and the small moments he carved out for himself—his workouts, his meals, even his bathroom breaks. I felt unappreciated by him, and he seemed to be living a stark contrast to my reality.

In truth, I was responsible for sweeping my needs under the rug.

TYPE 2—COMPASSION

The martyring caregiver had been lying dormant within me. The birth of my children unearthed this archetype, and I got lost in a vortex of my own "selfless" narrative. But I was the one blocking myself from the essence I needed—compassionate, embracing love.

I had innocently twisted this nurturing essence, turning it into survival traits—one-way streets that only led towards others and never back to myself.

True to the Type 2 in survival mode—I was becoming resentful, enraged. I expected my husband to read my mind and comprehend needs that I wasn't even consciously acknowledging.

My road to discovering this dynamic came with the support of a therapist. He held up a mirror to my life—he reflected my situation in a light I hadn't seen. Instead of perceiving my husband as neglectful, I came to realize that it was I who was neglecting myself.

I learned to hear my resentment as a wake-up call. Overtime, I gradually started to care for myself, nurturing my needs with some of the same tenderness I was giving my children. I learned to ask for help, to draw boundaries, and to grant myself moments of solace.

Want to know my biggest breakthrough?

I chose to learn from my partner rather than resent him for maintaining his health rather than becoming a martyr like me. In this self-centering process, I did not become less of a mother. Instead, I became more.

TYPE 2—COMPASSION

Motherhood unleashed the dormant Type 2 within me, but through embracing self-love, I found the balance between caring for others and caring for myself—a lesson I plan to pass down to my children.

My Type 2 journey was the key that helped me understand the multifaceted nature of personality. This was when I truly realized we are not just one type, but a kaleidoscope of all nine types.

We are not just one point on the Enneagram star. We are the whole circle around it.

Thank you for accompanying me on this nurturing journey. I hope my stories and insights have ignited deeper introspection within you.

Next, you'll find practical steps for embodying your Type 2 essence, designed to help you move beyond limiting personality traits and integrate this wisdom into your daily life. These resources are an *introduction* to the embodiment path — setting the stage for deeper explorations available in my full programs.

For a FREE printable copy of this embodiment guide for all 9 types, please visit my website: EnneagramofEssence.com

TYPE 2—COMPASSION

EMBODIMENT
PATH TO COMPASSION
EMBRACING TYPE 2 ESSENCE

JOURNEY INTO ESSENCE
The Enneagram of Essence's practical power is rooted in embodying essence and releasing limiting patterns. This brief guide to embodying Type 2's compassion is my gift, setting the stage for a much deeper exploration available in my full programs.

KINDNESS THROUGH TYPE 2 ESSENCE
Even though Type 2 is not my primary type, its essence nurtures and soothes me with kindness, offering a loving embrace within. *How could Type 2 essence enrich your inner and outer world?*

NATURE'S WARMTH
Consider the sweetness of a new relationship or the comfort of a sunlit beach. This is the soothing spirit of Type 2.

MIND-BODY WELLNESS
Mind-body research shows that self-love practices positively impact stress levels, enhancing well-being. Embracing self-nurturance builds inner contentment and deepens your relationships.

© 2023 Enneagram of Essence. All rights reserved.

Embodiment
Path to Compassion
Embracing Type 2 Essence

Step 1: Identify Portals To Compassion

Identify what ignites feelings of kindness for you — nature, memories, warm people, etc. For me, the idea of holding a soft, sweet animal evokes compassionate love.

What symbols or experiences spark inner compassion for you?

Incorporate elements like colors, textures, flavors, scents and sounds that mirror this quality into your space, as reminders of your Type 2 journey.

Step 2: Feel and Anchor Compassion

Notice the distinct way kindness and care feel within you. For me, connecting with this essence brings my heart a soft inner embrace, radiating a warmth akin to nurturing sunlight on a soft beach.

What does compassion feel like in your body?

Practice feeling and anchoring kindness deeply throughout your nervous system — visualize and feel it flow through you, influencing your posture, movements, and perceptions.

© 2023 Enneagram of Essence. All rights reserved.

TYPE 2—COMPASSION

Embodiment
Path to Compassion
Embracing Type 2 Essence

Step 3: Center Compassion

Make an effort to notice and value the essence of kindness and warmth in people around you. Focus on essence when noticing someone's personality.

Think about how centering this essence could change your understanding and appreciation of people with the primary Type 2.

How could this practice deepen your understanding and connections with people primarily identified as Type 2?

Step 4: Create a Practice

Incorporate these steps into a flexible and creative practice, bringing it into your daily routine from a week to a month. Focus on portals that ignite kindness and warmth. Through regular engagement, embodying inner compassion will become more and more effortless.

How will integrating these practices transform your daily life?

© 2023 Enneagram of Essence. All rights reserved.

Embodiment
Path to Compassion
EMBRACING TYPE 2 ESSENCE

Step 5: Abstain from Limiting Traits

Make space within yourself to cultivate compassion. Type 2 personality traits serve as survival mechanisms so it's important to release them gently, leaning on inner resources for support.

Mindfully identify and release Type 2 patterns that detract from your essence, including:

Overextending Yourself
Identify healthy boundaries. Caring for yourself as diligently as you do for others.

Ignoring Your Needs
Pay attention to and honor your body's signals. Let your heart's softness inform your choices.

Seeking Approval through Caregiving
Find self-validation rather than seeking it through acts of service. Anchor compassion within.

Avoiding Expressing Needs or Desires
Embrace the importance of sharing your needs and desires. Practice voicing your inner truths.

© 2023 Enneagram of Essence. All rights reserved.

TYPE 2—COMPASSION

> **EMBODIMENT**
> # Path to Compassion
> **EMBRACING TYPE 2 ESSENCE**

Step 5: Abstain from Limiting Traits

Mindfully identify and release Type 2 patterns that detract from your essence, including:

Passive-Aggressive Behaviors
Recognize and address indirect expressions of needs. Aim for warm yet direct communication.

Struggling with Saying No
Embrace saying no as part of healthy boundary-setting, supported by self-compassion.

Using Flattery to Gain Favor
Prioritize sincerity over charm in interactions. Remember to stay true to your genuine feelings.

Feeding Pride through Altruism
Stay mindful of the intentions behind your helpful actions. Ground yourself in authenticity.

Excessively Adapting to Others
Balance your responsiveness to others with a nurturing attention to your own needs.

Suppressing True Feelings
Acknowledge and express your emotions, use tools like journaling for emotional honesty.

© 2023 Enneagram of Essence. All rights reserved.

EMBODIMENT
PATH TO COMPASSION
EMBRACING TYPE 2 ESSENCE

STEP 5: ABSTAIN FROM LIMITING TRAITS
Mindfully identify and release Type 2 patterns that detract from your essence, including:

OVER-IDENTIFYING WITH CAREGIVING
Diversify your sense of identity and value beyond caregiving.

FOSTERING CODEPENDENCE
Encourage autonomy in others, respect their capacity to navigate their own journeys.

FEELING INDISPENSABLE
Accept the collective strength and capability of your community, recognizing your worth independently of your role as a helper.

Use Step 5 as a bridge, not fixed rules. By centering essence, your personality traits will naturally relax into the nourishing qualities of inner compassion, kindness and warmth.

Let's conclude with a moment of integration through this guided meditation—opening the door to inner kindness.

© 2023 Enneagram of Essence. All rights reserved

GUIDED MEDITATION FOR TYPE 2

I encourage you to find a comfortable position, relax your body, and gently soften your focus. Read this slowly and with ease, twice—first to visualize the imagery, and then again to deeply connect with the sensations it evokes.

Relax your gaze.
Take in a gentle, nurturing breath.

You find yourself
in the heart of a nurturing meadow.

Beneath your feet, the earth feels soft,
lush and supportive.

As dawn breaks, its golden light
envelops you in a gentle embrace,
whispering of life's tender care.

Around you, soft flowers bloom,
their petals swaying in the light.

The warmth of the morning sun
kisses your skin,
a soothing balm to your spirit.

In the heart of this meadow,
a warmth radiates.
A majestic tree stands tall,
its branches wide with welcome.

GUIDED MEDITATION FOR TYPE 2

*Approach it, feeling its presence
as a guardian of the land.*

*Beneath its canopy,
you find shelter, peace.*

*Leaning against its sturdy trunk,
the tree's embrace feels like coming home.*

*Its energy, ancient and wise,
seeps into you, filling every space
with comfort and care.*

Breathe in this moment,
allowing yourself to be cradled
by the arms of nature.

You are not alone.
The earth supports you.
the tree shelters you.

In this sacred space,
feel the deep connection.
A love that holds everything.

The nurturing meadow,
the protective tree,
the warming sun.

TYPE 2—COMPASSION

GUIDED MEDITATION FOR TYPE 2

In receiving nature's care,
you find the well of compassion within yourself
expands, embracing everything with warmth.

Here, in the embrace of the meadow,
you are both nurtured and nurturing,
a vital thread in the kind tapestry of life.

Pause for a moment.

How did that meditation feel? Could you sense the tenderness of the morning meadow and the warm care of the tree?

If that meditation resonated, it's because you accessed the *spirit* of compassion, beyond the external forms of life. The soft tree acts as a portal, yet the essence of compassion and kindness is an internal, intrinsic part of you.

This is your journey. Absorb these suggestions at your pace—let them take root. When you're ready, turn the page, we'll begin our journey into the power of your gut center, delving into the power that ignites us all.

WANT TO DEEPEN YOUR ENNEAGRAM ESSENCE JOURNEY?

Visit: EnneagramofEssence.com

You'll discover a wealth of resources designed to support wherever you are on the Enneagram path — explore our free resources, fundamentals course, podcasts, workshops, and a full accredited certification program.

YOUR GUT CENTER

GROUND OF YOUR BEING

POWER & ANGER

Have you ever experienced your gut center...

- As the strong "base" or steady "foundation" of your body?
- As a potency around, yet beyond, your impulses?
- As the powerful source that sparks your actions?

Take a moment to reflect.
Place your hands gently on lower belly.
Sense into this center of your being.

Ponder these questions, letting insights emerge naturally:

1. What kind of impulses arise most often within your gut?
2. What do these impulses feel like? Are they subtle or all-consuming?
3. How does your gut space differ from these passing impulses?
4. What sensations arise when you tap into the power of your gut center?
5. Are there specific moments when you really feel this powerful awareness?

6. What words describe this space—the *essence* of your gut center?

Allow these questions to linger in your awareness, giving yourself the time and space to explore them fully.

GUT CENTER ESSENCE — POWER

The essence of your gut center is power—not just personal strength, but a vital force that anchors your being. Imagine your gut's essence as the deep roots of a towering redwood, a foundational realm where autonomy, balance, and integrity grow strong and resilient.

This power emanates from your core, grounding and guiding your instincts, decisions, and actions. It's a realm where power extends beyond action—a source of true sovereignty, balance, and inner authority.

GUT CENTER EMOTION — ANGER

Your Gut Center is also the realm that wrestles with the fiery energy of anger and its relatives—irritation and frustration. This potent emotion, often misunderstood, can seem disruptive or destructive. It might manifest as a tempest that stirs within, threatening to unsettle your sense of harmony and control.

Yet, anger is not your adversary—when consciously acknowledged and channeled, it becomes a healing force.

It can ignite assertiveness and strengthen your sense of integrity. Consider anger as a thunderstorm that clears the air, leaving the landscape more vibrant and alive than before. It urges you to establish healthy boundaries, to stand up for your values, and to protect your wellness.

Underneath the surface flames of your anger lie the potent embers of true inner strength. I invite you to reframe every spark of frustration as a call to action, a summon to align more deeply with your foundational roots. By welcoming your anger as an ally, you allow it to fortify your spirit and deepen your resolve.

GUT CENTER PERCEPTION — INSTINCTUAL

In this realm, instincts are not mere impulses but the lens through which you perceive and experience the world and your place in it. Here you intuitively navigate life with an instinctual understanding that feels deeper than conscious thought. This intelligence informs your decisions and actions, giving you a gut feeling of being aligned. It's how you "just know" things, where your immediate reactions come from, and what helps you stand firm in your sense of self.

GUT CENTER SEEKS — AUTONOMY

The gut center is where you seek to live in congruence with your core values, aiming for integrity, balance, and autonomy. This center propels you to establish a powerful sense of self-determination, where decisions stem from an inner compass rather than external pressures. From here, you strive for equilibrium in life, maintaining your inner grounding even in the face of conflict.

GUT CENTER ENERGETIC DIRECTIONS

Type 1 (Inward): Your attention turns inward—deep into your gut for introspection. Here, impulses are refined and anger is honed to achieve integrity and actualize ideals.

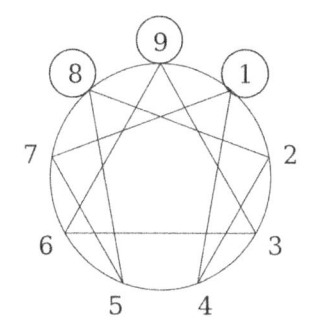

Type 9 (Balanced): Your attention is balanced—neutralizing extremes within and without. Anger is diffused

and impulses are adapted to cultivate harmony with the outer world and sustain peace within.

Type 8 (Outward): Your attention turns outward—towards the world for engagement. Impulses are amplified to express protective strength and anger is channeled into a robust drive for justice and leadership.

GUT CENTER PRACTICES AND TRADITIONS

Traditions and practices that tune into this center often work on grounding, empowering, and physical or somatic presence. Here are just a few examples.

Martial arts, rooted in various global traditions, are not just about physical defense but about harnessing and channeling your life force energy. Native spiritual practices like shamanic journeys lean into intuition, tapping into ancestral wisdom and the earth's grounding energy.

In modern wellness practices, grounding exercises and nature immersions are seen as avenues to connect with our primal instincts and gut feelings. It's about sensing the world around us, through our body, beyond thinking or feeling.

Examples:

- Martial arts
- Shamanic journeys
- Grounding exercises
- Nature meditation
- Herbalism

With this foundation for your gut center, let's conclude with a guided meditation. Immerse yourself in this portal into the essence of your gut center, the ground of your being.

GUT CENTER MEDITATION

I encourage you to find a comfortable position, relax your body, and gently soften your focus. Read this slowly and with ease, twice—first to visualize the imagery, and then again to deeply connect with the sensations it evokes.

Draw in a deep, nourishing breath.
Tune in to your gut center.

Feel the sensation of your gut,
your lower back and hips.
Find the space behind your navel.

Notice any tension.
Tenderly invite it to relax.

Notice the pulse of your intuition,
signaling right or wrong.

Picture your gut as a vast forest floor,
Sturdy, nurturing, and brimming with life force.

Within this space,
impulses flicker like embers,
shaping your actions.

Each impulse is distinct.
Each impulse is temporary.

GUT CENTER MEDITATION

Beneath these fleeting sparks,
is an ever-present, grounding potency.

Notice . . .
Most of the ground of your being
is steady, balanced, foundational.

Strong, resilient, enduring,
full of power,
purity, and integrity.

Feel its presence as a grounding force,
an anchor that's always available,
ready to guide and sustain you.

Pause for a moment.

How did that meditation feel? Did you experience the potent "ground" of your being?

If that meditation resonated, it's because you tapped into the ground of your being—the enduring force beyond your passing impulses. Remember, you do not need to control your instincts in order to experience the nourishment of your gut center.

GUT CENTER MEDITATION

With this foundation, let's explore the expressions of your gut center across its three types, starting with the deep refining power of Type 1, where purity and integrity interweave.

TYPE 1—INTEGRITY

PURITY & PERFECTION

KEY ELEMENTS

- **Center**—Body, Power, and Anger
- **Direction**—Inward Focus
- **Personality**—The Perfectionistic Reformer
- **Essence**—Integrity, Purity, Inner Perfection

Do you ever find yourself...

- Driven by a need to fix—yourself, others, the world?
- Compelled to call out when integrity is lacking?
- Fixating on the flaws in yourself and the world around you?

There is a facet of your personality that holds the disciplined nature of a Type 1. And even deeper, your essence holds its aligning nourishment.

TYPE 1—INTEGRITY

Have you ever felt...

- A profound acceptance even though the world seems flawed?
- That everything is unfolding within a universal perfection?
- A benevolent forgiveness for the imperfections around you?

Within each of us is the deep integrity of Type 1—a gut that craves a sense of alignment and responsibility in a world that seems to lack accountability. This essence is a portal to an inner perfection that is powerful enough to hold all of life's flaws.

Consider this a call to stop chasing perfection through judgment and criticism.

Instead, learn to embrace the flawed human experience and foster an inner integrity that goes beyond judgment. In doing so, you become an example of responsibility and forgiveness in a world fixated on criticism. Let me tell you about the part of me that resonates with Type 1.

THAT PART OF ME THAT JUDGES

> While Type 1 is not my primary type, I've learned how to draw from its strong, sturdy roots within. Whether Type 1 is a subtle hue in the spectrum of your personality or the color that defines your primary type, I hope my story inspires you to discover the Type 1 that resides within you.
>
> Type 1 played a key role in shaping my marriage dynamics during the tough early years of raising kids—my marriage felt the strain. My Type 1 tendencies aimed for parenting perfection, setting the bars so high they caused more stress than success.
>
> My unwavering approach not only impacted my relationship with our children but also started to shape my husband Ben's

dynamic with them. Ben stepped into parenthood embodying a natural balance of structure and flexibility, whereas I came in with rigid rules. My inflexibility, especially in the early days of our family life, put a strain on our interactions and impacted the bond he was building with our kids.

I recognized that the rigid personality traits emerging within me were clear expressions of Type 1. Understanding this, I knew the remedy lay in its essence—deepening my connection with *true* integrity. This introspection not only transformed my perspective but also made room for Ben to authentically embrace fatherhood. As we began to blend our distinct parenting approaches, a remarkable synergy emerged.

The key moment in this journey? It's a special one I'll reveal later—a moment that significantly altered our family's interactions and my insight into Type 1. First, though, let's get to know this influential type and its refining essence more closely.

Take a moment,
Ground through your gut,
Prepare to explore the depth.

WELCOME TO TRUE PERFECTION

Let's begin by finding the deep roots of Type 1 within your own gut. Imagine a beacon of integrity as steadfast as a lighthouse, anchored in your foundation.

It's as if you have a mature, responsible elder within you, grounded in an unwavering integrity—as pure as an ancient forest ecosystem.

TYPE 1—INTEGRITY

Imagine yourself in a state where integrity isn't just an attribute but something you inherently are. True integrity doesn't arise from your behaviors. It isn't about acting morally or perfecting yourself—it's a vital quality that resonates from your gut.

You arrived in this world with a natural, pristine integrity—like a pure river source at the top of a mountain. As you journeyed through childhood, facing trials and tribulations, your connection to essence became obscured, weakened. Stress activated the survival traits of Type 1,

This disconnect led you to develop a critical point of view and a drive for flawlessness, setting you on a irritating search for true integrity and virtue.

Now, the Enneagram is your personal guide, leading you away from these defensive traits and back to your intrinsic integrity—beyond virtuous actions. It shows you that your personality traits are not obstacles but beacons, illuminating your profound desire to reconnect with the pure essence of your being.

Let's explore the important relationship between the essence of Type 1 and its personality traits.

TYPE 1'S QUEST FOR INTEGRITY

Your Type 1 traits, honed by childhood stress, drive you to pursue an elusive perfection. While well-intentioned, these strategies lead you away from the nourishment of true integrity and perfection.

Feeling disconnected from this essence, you seek integrity through perfecting everything within and around you—your actions, beliefs, standards, values, and expressions. You aim for an idealistic standard of perfection, overlooking the intrinsic purity at your core.

This pursuit often leaves you feeling irritable and blinds you to the inherent perfection that exists within you, your loved ones, and life itself.

TYPE 1—INTEGRITY

Consider my own Type 1 journey. As a new mother, I fixated on an idea of perfect parenting. My rigid adherence to this ideal overshadowed the imperfect joys that come with caring for my children.

Are there moments when your pursuit of excellence gets in the way of appreciating life as it is?

Remember—the traits of the Perfectionistic Reformer are all innocent attempts to replicate its core essence.

Your drive for a flawless life is a reflection of a deeper desire for inherent perfection. Your critical focus on improving the world imitates the natural refinement and progressive evolution that life inherently embodies.

As we delve into each characteristic in the following sections, think about how they reveal a quest for the essence of true integrity.

Take a moment to ponder these questions:

1. Do you often strive for perfection? Why?
2. Do you often notice imperfections or flaws around you?
3. Do you ever feel irritated if things seem flawed?
4. Is there discomfort or a sense of being incomplete when you're not improving or correcting something?
5. How do you respond when your efforts to create order or correct flaws are overlooked or challenged?
6. When was the last time you experienced true integrity? Was it sparked by something outside or within you?

Let these questions sink in and return to them for deeper contemplation. Next, we'll explore the origins of Type 1 traits in your early life experiences.

CHILDHOOD OF TYPE 1 — ESSENCE TO FIXATION

Let's take a walk down memory lane, back to your childhood—viewed through the Type 1 lens. You may recall an earnest journey towards responsibility and purpose. Do you remember feeling like you were enrolled in some sort of rigorous training program for adulthood? Striving to get everything just right, even as a kid?

Whether at home, school, or within your community, you might have felt an overwhelming responsibility to ensure all things aligned perfectly. Perceived flaws around you may have ignited a yearning to smooth out all the wrinkles in the world.

What about the adults around you back then?

They might have seemed flawed to you, not living up to the standards you had internally set. Their imperfections seemed more like a source of irritation than an assurance of their humaneness.

Here's an interesting thing. Your drive for perfection didn't isolate you. Instead, it made you value relationships and institutions that upheld high standards. They became benchmarks of behavior and ethics that you strived to match—this has significantly shaped who you are today.

It's important to recognize that your diligence and discipline stem more from those early feelings of needing to grow up quickly. Your Type 1 personality is a response to stress, a survival strategy you developed to navigate the "imperfect" world you found yourself in.

Let's move beyond childhood and begin to unpack the details of the Perfectionistic Reformer.

TYPE 1—INTEGRITY

TYPE 1 NICKNAMES

The Perfectionist

You confronted the imperfections of the world early in life, cultivating a discerning eye for spotting flaws and an earnest desire to create order, improvement, and yes—perfection. In your view, there's always room for refining, enhancing, and making things just right.

Be it in your professional or personal life, you're relentless in your pursuit of excellence and adherence to high standards. Your dedication and intense commitment to integrity in all you do can feel like a burden. You are like a sculptor, painstakingly chiseling away at a stone until it mirrors your envisioned ideal.

The Reformer

You possess a keen awareness that the world can be better, fueling a deep passion within you. This isn't simply about discerning flaws—it's about envisioning ways to fundamentally improve the world around you.

Despite facing challenges, your unwavering commitment to reforming pushes you forward, positively shaping the world around you. A mature Type 1 balances traditional and progressive energies, making thoughtful decisions with integrity and driving innovation across various areas of life and work.

The Judge

You've always had an innate understanding of right and wrong, a deep sense of justice that drives you to assess, evaluate, and indeed—judge. This isn't just about being critical—it's about seeking balance, fairness, and setting things straight.

In your personal and professional life, you act as an arbiter of standards, persistently striving to uphold ethical guidelines and expecting the same from those around you. Although reforming your

TYPE 1—INTEGRITY

world poses a challenging responsibility, you are resolved, fortified by your commitment to truth and justice.

Quite a responsible role to play, wouldn't you say?

MEET LISA, WHO OVERSTEPPED IN HER PASSION FOR EXCELLENCE

> Lisa, a yoga teacher with the primary Type 1, sought therapy after leaving her teaching position at a studio. Despite good intentions, she overstepped her role as a part-time instructor. She and the studio owner disagreed on various operational aspects—from class start times to dress codes, water quality, and the brightness of the lighting.
>
> While Lisa tried to approach matters delicately, she was outspoken about her views.
>
> These unsolicited actions and opinions, while stemming from her desire to improve the studio, made staff and students uncomfortable. This led to conflicts and feelings of being burdened and misunderstood.
>
> Recognizing the essence of Type 1 as a perfect source of nourishment for Lisa's overbearing sense of responsibility, we focused on her connection to universal integrity. I introduced essence practices to help her find a forgiving acceptance of the perceived "imperfections" in her work environment.
>
> As Lisa embraced the essence of Type 1, she not only found relief from her inner critic but actually became a source of positivity to those around her.
>
> As her connection with true integrity and inner perfection grew, she found the flexibility to inspire improvements at her new job

TYPE 1—INTEGRITY

without overstepping boundaries. Most importantly, Lisa developed the ability to accept the "imperfections" of life.

These nicknames carry rich details, so let's dive into the primary traits associated with the Perfectionistic Reformer.

PERSONALITY TRAITS OF TYPE 1

Desire: To Be Good, Ethical, and to Have Integrity

Your personality is rooted in the desire to be exemplary and feel a deep sense of correctness. In addition, you want to bring order and perfection into every aspect of your life, personal and professional.

You are motivated by the desire to live in an impeccable manner and contribute positively to the world. Any slip-ups or mistakes feel profoundly painful—as they poke at your underlying fear of being imperfect and flawed.

Emotion: Irritation and Frustration (Internalized Anger)

The core emotion of your gut is anger. Being an inwardly focused type, you tend to repress, regulate, and pull anger in. You see anger as a flaw that is not included in your ideal of perfection—so you strive to suppress it.

But the intensity of your anger can't be fully repressed—it seeps out in subtler forms like annoyance and frustration. Your anger doesn't vanish—it just burrows deep within you, contributing to your stiff and upright posture. If you relate to feeling anxious—dig deeper and you'll find that it's often a response to your held-in anger.

Fixation: Judgment and Criticism

Your pursuit of perfection leads to a heightened sense of judgment, both towards yourself and others, especially when expectations aren't met. You constantly measure actions and behaviors against an internalized ideal. This tendency means that for every criticism you direct outward, there are often more directed inward.

This judgmental stance is not intended to harm but comes from a place of wanting to improve and reform. It's a constructive effort, albeit a critical one.

However, receiving criticism from others can be particularly challenging for you. It compounds the self-judgment you're already experiencing. Even feedback meant to help can be perceived as criticism through your judgmental lens, making it harder to accept without amplifying existing feelings of guilt and self-critique.

Shadow: Inner Flaw and Guilt

Lying in the shadows of your unconscious is a deep-seated fear of being corrupt or defective. When you fail to meet your own standards, you experience guilt and view yourself as inherently flawed.

The core coping mechanism for this shadow is through a process called "reaction formation." This is where you hide feelings or desires you think are unacceptable by acting in the exact opposite way. For instance, if you feel guilty about your perceived flaws, you might overly focus on being logical, in control, and perfect.

This helps turn unbearable emotions into behaviors that feel more appropriate and under control—allowing you to present a composed and virtuous front while wrestling with your "flawed" feelings internally.

MEET MARK, WHO OVERCAME HIS REACTION FORMATION

> Mark, a diligent Type 1 life coach, embodies a commitment to high ethical standards, a trait that is both admirable and a source of inner conflict. His relentless pursuit of perfection often left him feeling perpetually short of his own lofty

TYPE 1—INTEGRITY

expectations, giving rise to repressed anger and harsh self-criticism.

Yet, to the outside world, he maintained an impeccable facade of calm proficiency, a classic example of reaction formation where his external demeanor belied the turmoil within.

Our work focused on helping Mark acknowledge and accept his emotions, rather than pushing them aside. The goal was to show him that it was healthy to experience feelings of frustration or anger and that these emotions were natural to his identity, just as much as his inherent kindness and determination.

Through embodiment practices, Mark deepened his connection with essence. Gradually, he understood that he didn't need to be perfect to be helpful. He started to appreciate the inherent integrity embedded within life's imperfections. This new perspective enabled him to embrace and forgive his anger, softening his tendency towards reaction formation.

As a result, he cultivated a more compassionate view of himself, which naturally extended to a gentler, more authentic approach with his clients.

Mark's journey stands as a powerful example of the transformation that the Enneagram can bring. But what does Type 1 actually feel like from within? Let's dive into the sensations and experiences of this type in your body, exploring the intricacies of both its personality and essence.

SOMATIC EXPERIENCE OF TYPE 1

Energetic Direction—Inward

Compared to the other gut types—the Type 8 that turns outward or the Type 9 that balances—your Type 1 turns inward, delving into your inner ideals and deep sense of integrity. You aim to maintain a deep sense of integrity and correctness within yourself.

For instance, if you're asked at work to cut corners in a way that goes against your ethical standards, you'll reflexively pause to introspect. Despite potential external pressure to comply, you will prioritize aligning your actions with your strong sense of right and wrong.

In Stress—Reforming

On the outside, you stand rigid and poised, an emblem of precision. Your lips are often pursed from inward censoring and holding back critiques.

Inside, you're vigilant for any deviation from the ideal—each imperfection feels like a splinter in your gut. Deep within your belly, anger spirals, perfectly coiled and under control—ready to spring but held in check. Your heart beats to an orderly drum, and your spine aligns with rigid perfectionism.

A heaviness sits on your chest—a relentless pressure to always be right. Deep down, there's a burning desire for the goodness you seek, paired with a looming fear of every potential misstep.

With Essence—Embodied Integrity

As the rigid perfectionist relaxes, true integrity nourishes your being.

Externally, you still hold a solid stature but now with an absence of rigidity. Your poise feels grounded yet carries the lightness of acceptance.

Internally, the weight of self-correction dissipates—it's like the burden of the world has been lifted. Your structure is aligned yet flexible. Your

TYPE 1—INTEGRITY

belly is soft and accepting, while still strong with integrity and the confidence to speak your truth. Every breath feels light and cleansing, like inhaling the pristine winter air.

Now, as we venture into our last section, carry this innate goodness into understanding the mature Type 1.

MATURE TYPE 1 — FIXATION TO ESSENCE

Indeed, maturity in your Type 1 fundamentally comes down to nurturing inner integrity, beyond ideals or actions. The spirit of integrity is so all-encompassing, it transcends any standard and embraces both perfection and fallibility with the same deep power.

Envision yourself like a strong lighthouse staying aligned in the face of an irresponsible sea.

Remember your uncompromising drive for improvement?

It's evolved into an admirable ability to inspire others, without any added pressure. The driving force behind your work has shifted from seeking perfection to prove your goodness to an authentic expression of integrity—where your actions flow effortlessly from your true self and the perfection that underlies all things.

Let's talk about your relationships. They feel different now.

As you mature, your desire for integrity has led you to a real understanding and acceptance of others' viewpoints. You've discovered a new depth of connection.

Your integrity blossomed, becoming more nuanced, more compassionate. You've filled with patience and a genuine respect for everyone's unique journey.

You've developed a well-rounded understanding of what's truly good, right, and beneficial. You're not just an example anymore—you're an inspiration, a beacon of forgiveness and understanding.

TYPE 1—INTEGRITY

Quite a transformation, don't you think?

This doesn't mean you've stopped pushing for progress or making the world a better place—instead, you pursue improvement with a sense of profound appreciation. While your work no longer demands flawlessness, it still celebrates it.

With that, I'd love to wrap up this chapter by sharing more about my own journey with Type 1. Remember I shared about my early days of motherhood, filled with rigid standards? Now I'll share how I learned to relax those stringent guidelines with inner integrity.

I Realized My Rigidity Could Hinder the Bond Between My Children and Their Father

> In the early years of motherhood, I found myself entrenched in my Type 1 traits.
>
> Ben and I had just begun this incredible journey of raising our two little ones. I was filled with the conviction that I knew how we should parent, a certainty that stemmed from my deep desire to do everything perfectly.
>
> My approach was rigid and specific. Every word we spoke, every tone we used, and every aspect of our children's sensory diet—from screen time to food choices—fell under my purview.
>
> Ben's approach to parenting was different. He relied on instinct, adopting a more relaxed pace. Unlike me, he wasn't strict about screen time, diet, or medicine. Interestingly, his Type 1 essence was really evident in this realm—embodied in true integrity and an accepting attitude, confidently navigating parenting without the inner worry of making mistakes.
>
> My judgment about our differences strained the relationship between us and, unfortunately, started to affect Ben's

TYPE 1—INTEGRITY

interactions with our children. Always being scrutinized made him self-conscious and unnatural around our kids.

My wake-up call came when I realized my rigidity could hinder the natural bond between my children and their father. That's when I began working with the distinct nourishment of the Type 1 essence. I gave myself some breathing room from my perfectionistic traits, and with nourishment I began to appreciate the value in Ben's approach.

I came to see that his different style also had significant benefits for our children. His routines offered a different flavor of stability, and his ideas about sensory input and diet were grounded in their own logic and care.

In learning how to abstain from my rigid Type 1 tendencies—letting go of my need to control—I learned that our children thrived in ways I hadn't anticipated. Now they seem to enjoy the blend of my enthusiasm and Ben's stability. In this way, they get the best of both worlds.

Freed from my constant criticism, Ben could be himself around our kids, bringing his natural warmth and security to their lives.

By embracing my Type 1's true essence, I found that true integrity is not about imposing my views, but about respecting and appreciating others' perspectives. My pursuit of perfection transitioned from micromanaging to seeking a balance that serves my family's deeper needs.

In the end, my journey of healing my Type 1 traits led me to a place of forgiveness and acceptance. I learned that perfect parenting doesn't come from perfect standards, but from the ability to adapt, respect, and appreciate the diverse ways of expressing love and care.

Next, you'll find practical steps for embodying your Type 1 essence, designed to help you move beyond limiting personality traits and integrate this wisdom into your daily life. These resources are an *introduction* to the embodiment path — setting the stage for deeper explorations available in my full programs.

For a FREE printable copy of this embodiment guide for all 9 types, please visit my website: EnneagramofEssence.com

TYPE 1—INTEGRITY

Embodiment
Path to Integrity
Embracing Type 1 Essence

Journey into Essence
The Enneagram of Essence's practical power is rooted in embodying essence and releasing limiting patterns. This brief guide to embodying Type 1's integrity is my gift, setting the stage for a much deeper exploration available in my full programs.

Integrity Through Type 1 Essence
While Type 1 is not my primary type, its essence brings a nourishing sense of alignment and inner authority to my life. It acts like an inner pillar, aligning my mind, heart, and gut—instilling me with confidence and integrity. *How could Type 1 essence enrich your inner and outer world?*

Nature's Perfection
Consider the perfection found in the geometry of nature — the intricate design of a leaf or the symmetry of a snowflake. That's the aligning spirit of Type 1 — true perfection inherent in life.

Mind-Body Wellness
Research indicates that connecting with an inner sense of goodness and integrity can bolster resilience against stress, fostering a stable and accepting presence.

© 2023 Enneagram of Essence. All rights reserved.

Embodiment
Path to Integrity
Embracing Type 1 Essence

Step 1: Identify Portals To Integrity

Reflect on what evokes a sense of pristine goodness within you — the natural world, memories, certain individuals, etc. The geometry of a snowflake fills me with a sense of refreshing inner integrity.

What symbols or experiences spark integrity for you?

Incorporate elements like colors, textures, flavors, scents and sounds that mirror this quality into your space, as reminders of your Type 1 journey.

Step 2: Feel and Anchor Integrity

Notice the unique sensations of integrity and perfection within you. For me, connecting with this essence effortlessly aligns my posture, bringing my physical being into a sense of balance.

What does integrity feel like in your body?

Practice visualizing and feelings the sensation of integrity throughout your being. During critical moments, draw on your portals to integrity and reclaim your sense of inner purity and alignment.

© 2023 Enneagram of Essence. All rights reserved.

TYPE 1—INTEGRITY

Embodiment
Path to Integrity
Embracing Type 1 Essence

Step 3: Center Integrity

Make an effort to notice and value the essence of integrity and purity in people around you. Focus on essence when noticing someone's personality.

Think about how centering essence could change your understanding and appreciation of people with the primary Type 1.

How could this practice deepen your understanding and connections with people primarily identified as Type 1?

Step 4: Create a Practice

Incorporate these steps into a flexible and creative practice, bringing it into your daily routine from a week to a month. Focus on portals that ignite integrity and goodness. Through regular engagement, embodying true perfection will become more and more effortless.

How will integrating these practices transform your daily life?

© 2023 Enneagram of Essence. All rights reserved.

EMBODIMENT
PATH TO INTEGRITY
EMBRACING TYPE 1 ESSENCE

STEP 5: ABSTAIN FROM LIMITING TRAITS

Make space within yourself to cultivate integrity. Type 1 personality traits serve as survival mechanisms so it's important to release them gently, leaning on inner resources for support.

Mindfully identify and release Type 1 patterns that detract from your essence, including:

STRIVING FOR PERFECTION
Embrace imperfection as part of growth. Celebrate the natural perfection around you, finding balance between striving and being.

CRITICISM AND JUDGMENT
Cultivate understanding. Connect with the essence of true integrity in moments of judgment.

RIGIDITY
Foster flexibility and openness in thoughts and actions. Let the inherent perfection of adaptability remind you of life's flexibility.

IMPATIENCE
Practice patience through mindfulness. Sensory cues, like calming scents, can ground you in moments of restlessness.

© 2023 Enneagram of Essence. All rights reserved.

TYPE 1—INTEGRITY

EMBODIMENT
PATH TO INTEGRITY
EMBRACING TYPE 1 ESSENCE

STEP 5: ABSTAIN FROM LIMITING TRAITS

Mindfully identify and release Type 1 patterns that detract from your essence, including:

OVER RESPONSIBILITY
Share tasks. Remember to balance duties with self-care and compassion.

SUPPRESSING FEELINGS
Practice acknowledging and expressing your emotions.

AVOIDING RELAXATION
Prioritize activities that promote tranquility, such as tai chi, nature walks, or immersive reading, to ease into a state of calm.

FEAR OF MISTAKES
View mistakes as opportunities for growth. Remember the value in learning from imperfections and focus on the journey.

REACTION FORMATION
Strive for emotional honesty with yourself — take time to delve into your emotional layers.

RESENTMENT
Cultivate the strength and wisdom of forgiveness.

© 2023 Enneagram of Essence. All rights reserved.

Embodiment
Path to Integrity
Embracing Type 1 Essence

Step 5: Abstain from Limiting Traits
Mindfully identify and release Type 1 patterns that detract from your essence, including:

Fixating on Details
Dedicate time to broad-thinking or creative activities. Use affirmations to guide your focus away from perfectionism in details.

Struggle with Uncertainty
View uncertainty as an opportunity for self-nurturing. Remember the perfection within life's unpredictability.

Clinging to Idealistic Standards
Surround yourself with items that celebrate natural variance, reminding you of the value in embracing life's imperfections.

Use Step 5 as a bridge, not fixed rules. By centering essence, your personality traits will naturally relax into the nourishing qualities of integrity and purity.

Let's conclude with a moment of integration through this guided meditation—opening the door to inner perfection.

© 2023 Enneagram of Essence. All rights reserved.

TYPE 1—INTEGRITY

GUIDED MEDITATION FOR TYPE 1

I encourage you to find a comfortable position, relax your body, and gently soften your focus. Read this slowly and with ease, twice—first to visualize the imagery, and then again to deeply connect with the sensations it evokes.

Relax your eyes.
Take in a long, purifying breath.

You're standing in a pristine,
winter landscape.

Crisp, cold air
caresses your skin,
awakening your senses.

Inhale deeply.
Feel the crisp, purity
of the winter air
filling your lungs.

Before you,
an expanse of untouched snow,
glistening under winter light.

Step forward,
Hear the satisfying crunch
beneath your shoes.

© 2023 Enneagram of Essence. All rights reserved.

GUIDED MEDITATION FOR TYPE 1

*A sense of childhood
innocence and perfection
stirs within.*

*Listen . . .
The sound of purity
floating from the sky.*

*Snowflakes drift gracefully,
each holds an intricate design,
shimmering in the soft light.*

*Observe one closely,
admire its delicate form
and impeccable design.*

*In these delicate ice crystals,
you find life's inherent
elegance and intentionality.*

*Daily worries fade,
replaced by rejuvenation,
and renewal.*

*The snow flakes
uplift your spirit,
illuminating the perfection
woven into nature.*

© 2023 Enneagram of Essence. All rights reserved.

TYPE 1—INTEGRITY

GUIDED MEDITATION FOR TYPE 1

Pause for a moment.

How did that meditation feel? Could you sense the crispness of the winter morning?

If that experience resonated, it's because you accessed the *spirit* of integrity, which is not confined to external forms of life. The winter snow acts as a portal, yet the essence of purity and integrity is an internal, intrinsic part of you.

This is your journey. Absorb these suggestions at your pace—let them take root. When you're ready, turn the page with me to Type 9. Let's unveil the layers of peace and harmony that reside within you.

© 2023 Enneagram of Essence. All rights reserved.

TYPE 9—HARMONY

BALANCE & UNITY

KEY ELEMENTS

- **Center**—Body, Power, and Anger
- **Direction**—Balanced Focus
- **Personality**—Calm Peacemaker
- **Essence**—Harmony, Balance, Unity

Do you ever find yourself...

- Seeking comfort by "zoning out" with soothing activities?
- Stepping back from confrontation, choosing the comfort of agreeing?
- Prioritizing others' preferences to maintain a sense of harmony or unity?

There is a part of your personality that manifests the peace-seeking nature of Type 9. And beyond these traits, your essence is attuned to its harmonious nourishment.

TYPE 9—HARMONY

Have you ever felt...

- Grounded and present amidst intense emotions or disputes?
- A calmness that embraces all of life's tones, even conflict?
- A harmony that unites it all, even chaos and discord?

We've all got a Type 9 foundation within—a gut that seeks balance and harmony. We all need a sense of unity in a world that thrives on conflict and division. The essence of this type is a portal to an inner harmony that can hold *every* expression of life.

Consider this a call to stop chasing harmony by ignoring yourself.

Instead, foster an inner sense of unity that makes room for your own needs and preferences just as much as others'. By embracing this essence, you become an example of all-inclusive harmony and balanced power in a world fragmented by our differences. Let me tell you about the Type 9 in me.

THAT PART OF ME THAT MERGES

> While Type 9 does not dominate my personality, its influence has been one of the strongest in shaping my life. Whether Type 9 is the driving current or a gentle ripple in your makeup, I hope my story will inspire you to discover your own inner Type 9.
>
> Life is fluid, constantly in motion, changing its course. But have you ever felt like water, taking on new shapes and flows to harmonize with the energies of those around you? That's precisely my link to Type 9.
>
> In my friendships, I've often been like water in a vessel—taking the shape of the container it's poured into.

With my introspective friend Lora, our bond was like a calm lake under a starlit sky. While my vibrant friend Eliza and I were more like a cascading waterfall, energetic and unbridled. Whether I'm exploring nature trails with Leo or diving deep into emotional realms with Bliss, every connection has felt like a unique river, shaping and reshaping me.

But was this endless adapting truly natural? Or was I just adjusting my flow to match the stronger current? I've come to realize that sometimes I excessively streamline certain facets of myself, while accentuating others, all in pursuit of that harmonious connection—so characteristic of Type 9.

For me, Type 9 isn't just about specific moments. Instead of a "That Part of Me" story, it's a blended theme in my nature, one of the types I resonate with most.

So what happened to my sense of self in these relationships? How did I blend in to ensure the harmony I so deeply cherish? This chapter peels back the layers of these very questions.

How do relationships influence your sense of self?

Where do you draw the line between blending in and standing out? And most importantly, what does it truly mean to be harmonious in our connections? I'll share insights, struggles, and ways to tap into the true essence of harmony.

You'll find my full Type 9 story as we wrap up this chapter. For now, settle in, and let's begin an exploration into this truly powerful type.

Find your comfort spot,
Inhale deeply, and
Embrace the journey ahead.

TYPE 9—HARMONY

With Type 9's unique position in the Enneagram circle, marking both the beginning and ending, this chapter promises to be enlightening. Let's get started.

WELCOME TO TRUE HARMONY

The best way to begin this exploration is by sensing into the essence of Type 9 that's already within you. Nestled deep within your gut is a quality of harmony as grounding and powerful as gravity—drawing everything into a balanced and unified embrace.

It's like you have a grounded martial artist inside you embracing all the expressions of life from the beginning of time, whispering age-old tales of unity and oneness.

This harmony is more than an agreeable nature, it is rooted in an internal sense of balance—never swayed by external forces. Much more than a concept, this unity is an embodied experience, emanating from your very gut.

Imagine you're at a family dinner and everyone has different opinions about what to discuss or what to eat. In this scenario, instead of reflexively conforming to others' preferences or trying to please everyone, you steadily acknowledge your own views and choices. You express them clearly, maintaining a peaceful yet assertive presence. This is you, embodying the essence of unity from your gut—holding your individuality while enjoying the diversity around you.

Isn't this a powerful journey to begin?

You came into this world deeply connected with life's inherent oneness. However, life's intensities gradually veiled this natural harmony. Under stress, you shifted into survival mode, losing touch with true harmony and settling for the guise of a neutral, easy-going persona.

This shift led you to develop a superficial agreeability, masking your deeper feelings and desires in order to maintain external harmony.

Now, the Enneagram serves as a beacon, guiding you away from mere peace-making and towards an anchored, powerful harmony that holds intensity without neutralizing it. This strength comes from deep within, unshaken and real, ready to face life's toughest challenges. Let's delve into the fundamental relationship between the personality traits of Type 9 and its essence.

TYPE 9'S QUEST FOR HARMONY

Your Type 9 traits developed under childhood stress, pulling your attention away from inner essence, and prompting you to pursue harmony externally. You've been seeking harmony by leaning back into a passive stance, believing that unity comes from merging. Ironically, this sometimes amplifies the very discord you aim to avoid.

For example, when teaching an Enneagram class, I once hesitated to set appropriate boundaries with a student who shared excessively. In trying to keep the peace and avoid confrontation, I unintentionally disrupted the overall harmony of the group.

When I tap into my Type 9 essence, I draw upon the strength of true unity and balance. This empowers me to address challenges directly, guided by all-inclusive harmony, instead of letting my passive urge to dodge discomfort take the lead.

Can you recall moments when your need to avoid conflict overshadowed your desire to address something head-on?

Consider this—every trait of the Peacemaker is intertwined with its essence of universal harmony. Your accommodating nature mirrors the true unity of all things. Your tendency to avoid conflict is a reflection of a deeper yearning for a sense of universal balance and natural equilibrium.

TYPE 9—HARMONY

As we explore these traits in the next sections, consider how they fundamentally relate to their essence.

Take a moment to ponder these questions:

1. Do you ever blend in with others' opinions to avoid conflict? Why?
2. Do you avoid expressing your true desires? What might you be avoiding?
3. How do you typically react to conflict? Do you confront it or pacify it?
4. Does the comfort of routine ever limit your potential?
5. Do you ever feel disconnected from your own needs and priorities? Why?
6. When did you last feel true harmony? Was it sparked by something outside or within you?

Let these questions resonate within you and return to them for deeper contemplation. Now, let's turn back to childhood and understand how these traits began to manifest.

CHILDHOOD OF TYPE 9 — ESSENCE TO FIXATION

Think back through the lens of Type 9 to those childhood moments when all you wanted was a chill, drama-free day.

Remember wanting to fly under the radar, just so things stayed peaceful? Perhaps school, home, or even that neighborhood playground taught you that blending in was easier than sticking out.

Were you the kid who thought, "Why rock the boat?" even if it meant setting aside what you really wanted? Like agreeing to pizza for the fifth time that week because everyone else wanted it, even though you were secretly craving tacos.

Think about those adults in your life, the ones who should've been your champions. Sometimes, they unintentionally nudged you to go

TYPE 9—HARMONY

with the flow a bit too much. Maybe their own issues made them crave peace and quiet, and without meaning to—they passed that on to you.

This whole "avoiding the waves" thing made you super good at one thing—seeing everyone's side of the story. It's like you had this superpower of understanding where people were coming from, even if it meant sidelining your own views.

It was clear, being easy going drew people closer, rather than pushing them away. Now, you often find yourself as the anchor in many groups. People know they can count on you for a drama-free zone.

It's important to note that always playing the peacekeeper isn't truly how you are. It's a tool you picked up along the way when the world around seemed to whisper, "Let's keep things smooth, okay?"

With those memories in mind, let's dive deeper into the qualities that earned Type 9 the nickname of the Peacemaker.

TYPE 9 NICKNAMES

The Peacemaker

Ever notice that soothing aura you carry, as if you could diffuse a bomb with your soft eyes and smile? That's your Peacemaker charm. When people call you this, they're feeling that inherent sense of harmony and balance you radiate. This isn't merely about sidestepping conflict—it's a reflection of your deep-seated drive to understand, connect, and foster unity.

Your peaceful demeanor is an active embrace of the middle ground. And this doesn't just resonate externally—it mirrors an inner journey too. You crave your essence of oneness, where every moment flows in harmony. However, true harmony isn't about avoiding the storm—it's

TYPE 9—HARMONY

about reminding us, and yourself, that amidst chaos, there's a unity holding it all together.

The Mediator

Ever find yourself between two clashing opinions, trying to bridge the gap? That's your Mediator side stepping up. When people see this in you, they're seeing more than just a knack for compromise. They're feeling your innate drive to bring about unity. You have this powerful ability to see multiple sides of a story, to truly listen to the melodies and discords of every voice, and to blend them into one balanced symphony.

It goes beyond just problem-solving or diplomacy—it's your way of fostering a space where every perspective is honored. You're not just going through the motions of a peacemaker—you genuinely become the bridge, ensuring that in a sea of diverse opinions, everyone feels heard and understood.

Easygoing

In the whirlwind of life, you're the steady breeze, encouraging everyone to take a moment and just breathe. Yet, this easy going nature can sometimes lead you to avoid confrontations or shy away from necessary conflicts. You've mastered the art of "going with the flow," which, while beneficial in understanding life's rhythm, can at times border on complacency, making you miss out on actively shaping your own destiny.

This side of you isn't merely about passive acceptance—it's about profound adaptability.

However, there's a fine line between adaptability and letting life pass by without taking the reins. Your relaxed vibe isn't just for show—it's a testament to your deep understanding of life's ebbs and flows. But remember, amidst life's storms, while it's important to find your calm center, it's equally crucial to stand up and chart your course.

TYPE 9—HARMONY

This balance you seek mimics the essence of the flow state—but you can learn to immerse in the moment while still steering the direction.

MEET JOHN—A BEACON OF GENTLE TRANSFORMATION

From our very first session, John was a calming presence in my office. As one of my earliest clients in my private practice, our therapeutic journey has spanned an incredible 15 years and continues to unfold.

Though my practice has moved and evolved many times over the years, John has remained consistent—living in the same town, home, and job. He easily flows with the shifts in my practice, highlighting his characteristic Type 9 adaptability.

Our sessions took a deeper turn as we started unearthing the layers of John's subdued self. It was a revelation to see how significantly he had set aside his own needs and emotions to appease others. A gentle exploration led him to realize that working tirelessly in a draining job was taking a deep toll on his spirit. The more profound epiphany? John didn't even need that job. He had another, more fulfilling role he could pursue, offering not just sustenance but genuine joy.

As he began considering this change, he was terrified. Gradually, he empowered himself with inner strength. Making a bold move, he carefully stepped away from his corporate job for work that resonated more deeply with his spirit. Watching this transformation was deeply inspiring—as this once-passive individual began to radiate deeply-rooted confidence and purpose.

John's awakening left a profound mark on me. Observing him embracing his inner strength gave me a tangible sense of the

TYPE 9—HARMONY

immense, yet subtle, power inherent in Type 9. It reminds me of gravity—silent yet foundational, often unnoticed but profoundly influential.

For the Type 9, transformations are like deep roots quietly growing, unseen yet strong, eventually leading to a vibrant and visible bloom. These nicknames hold a rich tapestry of traits—let's get to know each one in detail.

PERSONALITY TRAITS OF TYPE 9

Desire: To Maintain Peace and Harmony

At the core of your being, there's a primary yearning for peace and harmony. This desire runs so deep that you find yourself sacrificing your own needs and desires to preserve the tranquility around you. You try to become one with your environment, and the people in it, by losing sight of your own aspirations, boundaries, and sense of self.

To avoid conflict and seek common ground, you step away from personal desires and blend seamlessly with others' needs and preferences. In your pursuit of unity, you forgot your own voice. Your work lies in nurturing your unique self as an important part of the harmonious equilibrium of the world.

Emotion: Complacency (Avoided Anger)

As the balance-orienting gut type, you seek to harmonize the anger that governs the gut center—neutralizing it into a passive flow state. Your key challenge lies in the tug-of-war between engagement and withdrawal. You often disengage or distance—physically, emotionally, and energetically. You try to maintain equilibrium by sidelining strong moments, leading to missed opportunities and dulled experiences. In this dance, anger is tucked away to avoid disturbing the harmony you hold dear.

Although complacency is your recurring theme, you have the depth to feel so much more. Embracing the full spectrum of emotions will lead to a richer, more authentic harmony in your life. True unity means acknowledging and embracing your connection to anger. Rather than sidestepping it, make it a meaningful note in your life's symphony.

Fixation: Seeking Comfort

Your desire for comfort often translates into routines and habits that ensure minimal disturbance. This fixation can make you resistant to change, even if it's beneficial, because the known feels more comfortable than the unknown. Avoiding disruptions might feel safe, but it can also limit your growth and experiences. You find yourself defaulting to what's easy or familiar, avoiding confrontations, or procrastinating on decisions.

To nurture your authentic self, consider stepping outside your comfort zone, embracing change, and allowing yourself to experience the full spectrum of life's offerings.

Shadow: Disconnection

You step away from your own authenticity—disconnecting from your desires, needs, and preferences—in an effort to keep the outer world balanced. This creates a gap between your true self and the persona you present to the world.

Your tendency to avoid conflicts by going along with others' wishes might seem like a selfless act, but over time, it can foster a sense of resentment and internal disconnection. This pattern keeps you from fully engaging with your own presence and the people around you on a deeper level. To break free from this shadow, it's crucial to reconnect with your inner desires and recognize that asserting them doesn't disrupt harmony, but enriches it.

TYPE 9—HARMONY

MEET SUE, WHO FOUND HER VOICE

Our friendship began in our shared office at the Veterans Administration. Amid the demanding role of social workers, Sue and I found a kinship, navigating both the poignant stories of veterans and the tangled bureaucracy. Quiet Sue, with her gentle nods and soft-spoken demeanor, was a background figure. Had it not been for our common work, I would have never have glimpsed the universe that was Sue.

The pressures of our job inadvertently wove threads of connection between us. Finding humor, solace, and a sounding board in one another, our professional camaraderie seamlessly shifted into a personal bond.

Yet, I began to crave more.

At first, Sue's agreeable nature, her lack of resistance to any idea I brought forth, was comforting. But over time, it felt too one-dimensional. I sensed an undercurrent, a suppressed self beneath her placid surface.

One weekend we got together and I posed a challenge. "Sue, choose what we do this time."

Pushing Sue for her preferences wasn't easy. At first, she evaded, murmuring, "I genuinely enjoy whatever you pick—it's all good to me," clinging to her familiar safety of blending in. I had to express my growing frustration with always taking the lead, yearning for a balance in our choices. When she finally opened, her selections surprised me—far from my usual go-tos. I got to experience a new bookstore, a quirky diner, and a more vibrant, authentic Sue.

To many, such shifts might seem inconsequential. But for those who know the intricacies of a Type 9's psyche, it's monumental. This wasn't merely about selecting a diner—it marked Sue stepping into her own, infusing our dynamic with a newly charged synergy.

Embracing her individuality didn't just add zest to our time off—it reshaped the very fabric of our friendship, underscoring that with Type 9, subtle surface changes reflect palpable evolutions below.

Sue's journey illustrates the Type 9 facet that resides within us all. But what does Type 9 actually feel like from within? Let's dive into the sensations and experiences of this type in your body, exploring the intricacies of both its personality and essence.

SOMATIC EXPERIENCE OF TYPE 9

Energetic Direction: Balanced

Compared to the other gut types—the Type 8 that turns outward and the Type 1 that turns inward—your Type 9 seeks to balance and harmonize your actions and responses with the external world—the societal flow or pace. You want your actions and responses to align with the predominant harmony and flow of your chosen group or culture.

For example, in a team that values innovation and fresh ideas, you might amplify your creative suggestions, embracing a more vibrant, idea-driven persona to align with the team's dynamic energy. In contrast, in a community that cherishes tranquility and reflection, you might tone down your natural exuberance, opting for calm, thoughtful interactions to resonate with the serene atmosphere.

TYPE 9—HARMONY

In Stress: Peacemaking

Externally, there's a hint of withdrawal, with an inclination to blend in. Your breathing feels slow—each breath is a quest for harmony. There's an ever-present sense of inertia, making you feel grounded but sometimes too settled, static. The energy around your heart feels heavy, like navigating a day that demands more than you have to give. When faced with disruptions or confrontations, you pull back energetically, a protective reflex. Deep down, there's a longing for a world that moves at a gentler pace.

With Essence: Embodied Harmony

As the weight of inertia fades, you feel a renewed presence. Your breath deepens, steady like the rhythm of ocean waves. Your mind sharpens, pushing distractions aside to reveal what truly matters. Energy from your gut grounds you in the moment, while your gaze, still calm, now hints at a deeper understanding and empowerment. Each movement, like a river's determined flow, becomes deliberate and purposeful.

Soak in this awakened presence, allow it to usher you forward—let's get to know the Type 9 in its full, mature potential.

MATURE TYPE 9 — FIXATION TO ESSENCE

Your Type 9 evolution is about expanding your inner harmony to include your unique, empowered self. It's about finding empowerment *within* unity and embracing your individuality as an essential part of collective harmony.

Imagine yourself as a mature gravitational center, like a planet in orbit. You hold everything in a harmonious embrace—reflecting the power of universal diversity.

Remember your tendency to disconnect and avoid conflict?

TYPE 9—HARMONY

It's matured into a grounded authenticity. Now, you engage with life's ebb and flow with an empowered presence, confidently facing challenges while maintaining your inner balance and harmony.

Decisions feel different now. No longer overwhelmed by the desire to merge and appease, you confidently make choices aligned with your genuine desires. Your reluctance to assert yourself has transformed into a gentle strength—a willingness to express your preferences without fear of disturbing the waters of harmony.

Your search for external comfort has evolved into a journey toward inner harmony. You now find solace not just in external circumstances but in a deep-seated sense of inner balance. This new perspective allows you to embrace life's unpredictability, secure in the knowledge that true stability comes from within. As a result, you engage with the world more openly and adventurously, relying on your inner strength to navigate through varying situations.

And, what about your relationship with anger?

Once a suppressed and misunderstood aspect of your being, anger now serves as a gateway to deeper self-awareness and empowerment. Now, you recognize that anger is not something to be feared or denied, but a vital part of your gut center, a spark igniting the essence of universal power within you.

When anger surfaces, you invite it in and curiously listen to what it's trying to tell you—often, it points towards unmet needs or areas where your boundaries are being tested or need reinforcement. By tuning in, you've gained insights into where your strength is needed most, both for self-protection and in standing up for others. This empowered approach paves the way for anger to become a constructive force in your life, guiding you towards greater self-understanding and assertive, yet compassionate boundary-setting.

It's been an empowering journey, hasn't it?

TYPE 9—HARMONY

You're still you though, maintaining your serene demeanor, but now it's a reflection of inner harmony rather than a diffused mask to avoid conflict. Your ability to embrace all emotions—including anger—is a testament to your growth and courage.

With that, I'd love to end by sharing more about my Type 9 journey. Remember how I took on the traits of my different friends? Now, I'll show you how I learned to hold on to my truth, even faced with differing perspectives from those close to me.

MAJOR FACETS OF WHO I TRULY AM REMAIN UNSEEN BY THOSE CLOSEST TO ME

> Sunlight streamed through the window of the ice cream parlor, where I shared scoops and memories with my oldest friend, Lora. Our conversation, soft and reminiscent, took me back to our shared childhood—with whispered secrets and quiet dreams. Lora was a gentle introvert, and in her company, I felt a similar sense of reserved peace. I recalled the smooth beads we'd string together, crafting necklaces and bracelets, lost in our world of gentle introspection.
>
> High school introduced me to Eliza, a whirlwind of effervescence and vivacity. Life with her was a vibrant tapestry of hip hop beats, unapologetic dancing, and late-night culinary adventures. She kindled a wild flame within me, broadening my horizons in exhilarating ways.
>
> My friendships have left unforgettable marks on my journey.
>
> Leo, a nature enthusiast, inspired me to embrace the mountain waterfalls and the thrill of climbing tall trees. And then there was Bliss, the wellness guru. With her, I delved into women's ceremonies, deep meditations, and retreats with mystical plant medicines.

TYPE 9—HARMONY

Reflecting on it, I realize that my effortless tendency to merge aligns with the characteristics of Type 9—seamlessly blending with the vibes of those close to me. This isn't about putting on a mask or borrowing another's personality—these shifts are genuine elements of myself. Yet, in this process, I dim other authentic parts of myself to harmonize more closely with a friend. So much so, that major facets of who I truly am remain unseen by those closest to me.

With wisdom from the essence of Type 9, my discernment has deepened. I've grown attuned to moments when I dim my authentic self to align with another's rhythm. The nourishing essence of Type 9 teaches me about a deeper harmony that interweaves individuality with unity, reshaping the way I engage with those around me.

At a recent tea ceremony with Bliss, she steered our conversation deep into existential realms. As I was carried by her intense currents, a yearning for light-heartedness emerged. Braving the divergence, I infused the discussion with stories from my week and sprinkled in levity amidst the depth. Though I feared disturbing the deep ambiance, I was validated when Bliss later voiced her appreciation for the balance I brought.

This example is subtle on the surface. But for me, it was a game-changer. It validated that when I embrace my true self, my connections thrive not divide.

We await grand awakenings, but the real magic often lies in these small shifts. These tiny adjustments lead to profound internal transformations, echoing through our nervous system and reshaping our neural pathways.

Thank you for accompanying me on this balancing journey. I hope my stories and insights have ignited deeper introspection within you.

TYPE 9—HARMONY

Next, you'll find practical steps for embodying your Type 9 essence, designed to help you move beyond limiting personality traits and integrate this wisdom into your daily life. These resources are an *introduction* to the embodiment path — setting the stage for deeper explorations available in my full programs.

For a FREE printable copy of this embodiment guide for all 9 types, please visit my website: EnneagramofEssence.com

EMBODIMENT
PATH TO HARMONY
EMBRACING TYPE 9 ESSENCE

JOURNEY INTO ESSENCE
The Enneagram of Essence's practical power is rooted in embodying essence and releasing limiting patterns. This brief guide to embodying Type 9's harmony is my gift, setting the stage for a much deeper exploration available in my full programs.

UNITY THROUGH TYPE 9 ESSENCE
Even though Type 9 is not my primary type, its essence grounds me, connecting me to life's core balance and flow. *How could Type 9 essence enrich your inner and outer world?*

NATURE'S STILLNESS
Consider the stability you feel with your bare feet planted firmly on the earth or the calm that washes over you when you take a deep, conscious breath—this reflects Type 9's resilient spirit.

MIND-BODY WELLNESS
Mind-body research shows that nurturing an inner sense harmony affects stress responses, enhancing well-being — not only calming your nervous system but also deepening your sense of connection with others.

© 2023 Enneagram of Essence. All rights reserved.

TYPE 9—HARMONY

EMBODIMENT
PATH TO HARMONY
EMBRACING TYPE 9 ESSENCE

STEP 1: IDENTIFY PORTALS TO HARMONY

Identify what ignites feelings of harmony for you — nature, memories, calming people, etc. For me, envisioning birds flying in unison brings a sense of inner oneness and unity.

What symbols or experiences spark harmony for you?

Incorporate elements like colors, textures, flavors, scents and sounds that mirror this quality into your space, as reminders of your Type 9 journey.

STEP 2: FEEL AND ANCHOR HARMONY

Notice the distinct way balance and unity feel within you. For me, connecting with this essence brings a gentle strength from my gut, balancing and calming my being, as if syncing with life's steady rotation.

What does balance feel like in your body?

Practice feeling and anchoring harmony deeply throughout your nervous system — visualize and feel it flow through you, influencing your posture, movements, and perceptions.

© 2023 Enneagram of Essence. All rights reserved.

Embodiment
Path to Harmony
Embracing Type 9 Essence

Step 3: Center Harmony

Make an effort to notice and value the essence of harmony and unity in people around you. Focus on essence when noticing someone's personality.

Think about how centering essence could change your understanding and appreciation of people with the primary Type 9.

How could this practice deepen your understanding and connections with people primarily identified as Type 9?

Step 4: Create a Practice

Incorporate these steps into a flexible and creative practice, bringing it into your daily routine from a week to a month. Focus on portals that ignite harmony and unity. Through regular engagement, embodying true harmony will become more and more effortless.

How will integrating these practices transform your daily life?

© 2023 Enneagram of Essence. All rights reserved.

EMBODIMENT
PATH TO HARMONY
EMBRACING TYPE 9 ESSENCE

STEP 5: ABSTAIN FROM LIMITING TRAITS

Make space within yourself to cultivate harmony. Type 9 personality traits serve as survival mechanisms so it's important to release them gently, leaning on inner resources for support.

Mindfully identify and release Type 9 patterns that detract from your essence, including:

AVOIDING CONFLICT
Engage in constructive conflict for growth, use it to deepen your sense of *all-inclusive* harmony.

SUPPRESSING DESIRES
Recognize and prioritize your needs through somatic meditation — reflect on ignored desires.

NEGLECTING BOUNDARIES
Work to establish firm boundaries — use boundaries the enhance your inner harmony.

DEFERRING TO OTHERS
Practice sharing your opinions. Use symbols to remember your vital place in the world.

DENYING INNER ANGER
Listen to your anger to identify needs and set boundaries, see it as a powerful, guiding emotion.

© 2023 Enneagram of Essence. All rights reserved.

Embodiment
Path to Harmony
Embracing Type 9 Essence

Step 5: Abstain from Limiting Traits
Mindfully identify and release Type 9 patterns that detract from your essence, including:

Over-Accommodating
Pause in meeting others' needs — encourage them to tend to their own.

Ignoring Discomfort
Pay attention to and care for your body's signals — dedicate a space to harmony and self-tuning.

Avoiding Assertiveness
Cultivate assertiveness — ground in true harmony and find a balanced approach to speaking up.

Neglecting Self-Expression
Assert your thoughts and wear something bold as a reminder to express your true self openly.

Neglecting Personal Goals
Treat your goals with importance, use inertia as a cue to reconnect with balance and take action.

Resisting Change
Open to new experiences, seeing change as a path to growth. Let your inner harmony guide you through transitions.

© 2023 Enneagram of Essence. All rights reserved.

TYPE 9—HARMONY

EMBODIMENT
Path to Harmony
EMBRACING TYPE 9 ESSENCE

Step 5: Abstain from Limiting Traits

Mindfully identify and release Type 9 patterns that detract from your essence, including:

Choosing Complacency
Challenge complacency with active engagement, like martial arts, to inspire growth.

Minimizing Problems
Remember the importance of addressing issues — confrontation can lead to resolution.

Procrastination
Set goals, take action, keep motivated — proactive action enhances inner harmony.

Use Step 5 as a bridge, not fixed rules. By centering essence, your personality traits will naturally relax into the nourishing qualities of inner harmony, unity and balance.

Let's conclude with a moment of integration through this guided meditation—opening the door to inner unity.

© 2023 Enneagram of Essence. All rights reserved.

GUIDED MEDITATION FOR TYPE 9

I encourage you to find a comfortable position, relax your body, and gently soften your focus. Read this slowly and with ease — first to visualize the imagery, and again to connect with the sensations it evokes.

Relax your eyes.
Take in a slow, deep breath.

Imagine yourself as a bird.
Gracefully soaring
within a harmonious flock.

Feel the rush of air
under your wings,
a synergy of strength and grace.

Your heart beats in unison
with the flock,
each bird is an extension of yourself.

Below, the earth unfurls—
Sense its balance,
echoing in your flight.

Inhale deeply.
The cool, crisp air
fills your lungs,
heightening your senses.

© 2023 Enneagram of Essence. All rights reserved.

TYPE 9—HARMONY

GUIDED MEDITATION FOR TYPE 9

To your left,
companions glide effortlessly.
Movements of intuition
and instinct.

To your right,
the flock shifts and turns,
a fluid expression of unity.

Above, the boundless sky cradles you,
Its vastness resonates
with your inner sense of oneness.

Feel this harmony.
All-encompassing.
Profoundly natural.

Each bird intuitively knows its place,
Each contributing to a greater purpose.

Feel . . .
The intensity of your heart beat.
The unity of your flock.

Your individuality shines.
Yet you are seamlessly
one with the flock.

© 2023 Enneagram of Essence. All rights reserved.

GUIDED MEDITATION FOR TYPE 9

*In every synchronized glide and turn,
you are transformed.*

*A being of profound harmony.
Connected individuality.*

*Embrace an all-encompassing,
intuitive connection with life.*

Pause for a moment.

How did that meditation feel? Could you tune into the harmonious rhythms of the flock?

If that meditation resonated, you touched upon the *spirit* of unity and balance that resides within. The harmonious dance of a flock of birds serves as a gateway, yet true harmony is an internal, intrinsic part of you

Revisit any section as you wish and savor your personal insights. Once you feel anchored, turn the page. I am eager to guide you through our last type—the truly riveting world of Type 8.

© 2023 Enneagram of Essence. All rights reserved.

TYPE 8—STRENGTH

JUSTICE & EMPOWERMENT

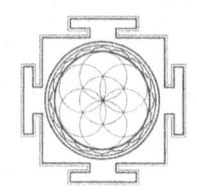

KEY ELEMENTS

- **Center**—Body, Power, and Anger
- **Direction**—Outward Focus
- **Personality**—Challenging Protector
- **Essence**—Strength, Justice, Inner Empowerment

Do you ever find yourself...

- Fiercely protective for those you care about?
- Taking a stand for your values with a commanding presence?
- Wanting to enact revenge when faced with injustice?

There is a part of your personality that has the assertive nature of Type 8. Even deeper, your inner essence holds its nourishing qualities of strength and vitality.

TYPE 8—STRENGTH

Have you ever felt...

- An inner strength that feels greater than your personal abilities?
- That your resilience runs deeper than your determination?
- A sense of universal justice, beyond your personal ideas?

Within each of us is the radiant power of Type 8—a core that craves justice and innocence. A longing for protection in a world that seems brutal. The essence of this type is a doorway to an inner power that embodies potency and tenderness equally.

Consider this a call to stop chasing justice by taking charge and confronting.

Instead, nurture an inner resilience that balances assertiveness with the grace to step back and trust universal justice. By embracing this essence, you become an example of true empowerment and humility in a world that challenges our resolve. Let me tell you about the Type 8 side of myself.

THAT PART OF ME THAT ROARS

> The inner strength and determination of Type 8 play a significant role within me, despite not being my primary type. By sharing my journey with Type 8, I hope to inspire you to discover and integrate these qualities in yourself, whether they represent a quiet spark or a guiding flame.
>
> Type 8's energy in me manifests as a powerful roar of protective force—an unwavering drive to rectify injustices. This profound "mama bear" instinct, though empowering, has at times led me to neglect my own need for vulnerability and the deeper needs of those dear to me.

TYPE 8—STRENGTH

Reflecting on my life, I find a pivotal moment where the presence of Type 8 was unmistakable. A close childhood friend suffered an injustice that left her emotionally devastated. Driven by a deep-seated need to protect and seek justice for her, my Type 8 instincts took center stage.

Compelled to confront the source of her pain, I was ready to fight, to ensure accountability. *My* overwhelming desire for retribution seemed like the right response, but it blinded me to what my friend truly needed.

She didn't need vengeance — she needed comfort, understanding, and the reassuring presence of someone who cared. In my pursuit of justice, I overlooked the importance of being there for her in the way she truly needed.

This chapter delves into the instinct to protect and challenge and the insights I've gained about the essence of Type 8's strength. True power extends beyond the battlefield — it's about being an open-hearted presence for those we love in a manner that truly supports them. Often, this means pausing our action-oriented instincts to offer gentle support and understanding.

These experiences have taught me the critical balance between strength and vulnerability, emphasizing the need to attune to the needs of those we hold dear.

By the end of this chapter, I'll return to that full story, marked by courage, loss, and deep learning. It's a journey that demonstrates how embracing our entire emotional spectrum, including our vulnerabilities, empowers us to exert our influence most effectively.

Now, let's delve deeper into understanding Type 8.

TYPE 8—STRENGTH

Take a moment.
Ground yourself.
Prepare to ascend.

WELCOME TO TRUE EMPOWERMENT

Let's begin by tapping into the resilient strength you have within, thanks to the essence of Type 8. Picture it like a strong, steady flame in the center of your gut, lighting up not just you, but also those around you—fueling an unwavering force to do what's right.

It's like you have an inner guardian—bold enough to stand up and protect, yet humble enough to know when to step aside and be vulnerable.

Imagine a version of yourself where standing for the truth feels as simple and natural as breathing. Not because someone's watching, but because it's just who you are. It's a kind of justice that goes beyond actions or words—it's a quality that fills every fiber of your being.

For example, imagine you're in a meeting where a colleague is being unfairly blamed for a mistake. Without hesitation, you speak up to clarify the situation, defending the truth simply because it's the right thing to do. This act, driven by your inner sense of justice, is a natural expression of who you are.

Feels enlivening to imagine, doesn't it?

You began life with this natural spark—a flame that was growing steadily year by year. However, life's challenges, like strong winds, caused this flame to burn too intensely. Stress pushed your Type 8 into survival mode, weakening your connection to inner power.

TYPE 8—STRENGTH

This shift resulted in an exaggerated expression of assertiveness and independence, propelling you on an unyielding quest for justice and strength.

Here's where the Enneagram can become your friend with a guiding light, leading you back to your authentic, empowered self—a self who embodies strength *and* tenderness. This journey is about more than external displays of strength—it's about uncoupling your notions of justice and power from mere ideas and actions, cultivating them from within.

Imagine waking up each day feeling empowered, ready to face challenges, savor simple moments, and embrace vulnerability with open arms. Let's delve into the fundamental relationship between the personality traits of Type 8 and its essence.

TYPE 8'S QUEST FOR JUSTICE

Your Type 8 traits formed under childhood stressors, pulling your focus away from inner essence, and prompting you to pursue strength externally. You've been seeking true power, justice, and resilience by constantly confronting challenges and fighting causes.

Assertiveness, leadership, and control became your method of protection and justice—ensuring you and those you love won't be taken advantage of. However, the act of maintaining control overshadows the importance of vulnerability and tenderness in your connections.

This external search keeps you in a constant state of defensive vigilance. It obstructs your ability to feel the true source of power and justice within you. Take my story for example.

When my close friend was hurt, my immediate reflex wasn't to console, but to seek revenge. The injustice was like a burning flame, compelling me to face the offender head-on. In retrospect, the true strength in that situation would have been to stay beside my friend, providing nurturance and support.

Are there times where your defensive nature blocks you from the genuine justice that you and those around you deserve?

My impulse to react with anger and seek retribution overshadowed my capacity for empathy. My friend needed nurturing during that time. A more grounded approach, blending strength with tenderness, would have better served the situation.

Every trait of the Challenger is a reflection and imitation of power and justice. Your drive to stand up for others and fight for what's right mirrors the universe's natural balance and fairness. Likewise, your display of strength and apparent invulnerability echoes life's deeper resilience and fundamental innocence.

As we delve further into this personality, I encourage you to reflect on how each trait might represent a deeper yearning for the essence of power and justice.

Take a moment to ponder these questions:

1. Do you ever find yourself asserting control in situations? When and why?
2. Do you ever feel a strong urge to protect others? How does this manifest?
3. Do you ever struggle with feeling or showing vulnerability?
4. How do you respond when you perceive a lack of fairness or justice?
5. Do you find it challenging to ask for help or support?
6. When did you last feel true strength? Was it sparked by something outside or within you?

Let these questions resonate within you, and return to them for deeper contemplation. Now, let's visit the origins of this protective personality—your early years.

TYPE 8—STRENGTH

CHILDHOOD OF TYPE 8 — ESSENCE TO FIXATION

Reflect on your early years through the lens of Type 8. Your world may have seemed like an arena—family conflicts, friends' challenges, community issues, and authority figures dictating the rules. There you were, amidst the chaos, a young pillar of strength and determination.

You began to hear the silent code—to be respected means to be strong, to be acknowledged means to stand your ground.

In school, you were the one classmates could turn to when facing adversity. They knew if someone was picking on them or if they needed backup, you'd be there. There was a unique protection in your presence.

But who stood up for you? Who had your back?

Who was there to listen to your vulnerabilities, to acknowledge your feelings, to support your aspirations? While defending and empowering others, your own inner world became a quiet echo. You learned that respect and safety were often tied to demonstrating power and control, to never showing weakness.

Yet, deep within, you craved acknowledgement for more than your strength, an understanding that recognized your tender moments and the heart that drove your fierce protection.

This is the origin of the protector in you, a power emerging from a limited understanding of respect and strength. Now, you're on a journey to discover an inner power that protects and cares for you.

It's time to step out of the past and get to know the most important characteristics of the Challenging Protector.

TYPE 8 NICKNAMES

The Protector

You have a remarkable capacity to stand up for others, advocating for those who cannot defend themselves. Since childhood, you've acted as a shield against injustice, boldly taking a stand when others might hesitate or back down.

This quality, rooted in a need for respect and justice, characterizes much of your interactions. You are often the first to defend friends, support family, or challenge any perceived threats, always ensuring protection and safety.

However, this protective stance can be overbearing, leading to unnecessary confrontations. It's important to balance this inclination with discernment, to ensure that your efforts don't inadvertently create conflicts or miss opportunities for growth through humility and vulnerability.

The Challenger

From your early days, your identity interlinked with a need to challenge the status quo—developing an intuitive ability to question, confront, and drive change. This trait goes beyond merely defying norms—it's rooted in your strong convictions about justice and fairness.

Your assertiveness, often perceived as aggressiveness, originates from a passionate desire to create positive change and foster justice. This willingness to step into the fray, challenging and reshaping power dynamics, stems from a deep-seated desire for a world that is balanced and just.

The Leader

You possess the charisma and drive to guide others, always taking the helm in situations that require direction. Your leadership spirit is

TYPE 8—STRENGTH

unwavering, steering those around you towards shared goals and mutual success.

You uplift and embolden, inspiring others to embrace their own strength and potential. People gravitate towards you, seeking both guidance and encouragement. As you pave the way for others, remember the importance of balancing your desire to challenge with your need for tenderness and vulnerability.

It's truly an admirable role to hold, wouldn't you say?

MEET PROFESSOR JONES, A BEACON OF TRUTH AND JUSTICE

Let's delve into the life of Mr. Jones, my Anthropology professor who was the full embodiment of Type 8.

With a presence that commanded respect, Professor Jones radiated leadership in its truest form. Every lecture he delivered, every story he shared, was punctuated by his bold commitment to truth and justice. He didn't just impart knowledge—he activated it within us.

I couldn't help but deeply admire him for his conviction and bravery.

His audacious dissertation research into the Ku Klux Klan wasn't just an academic endeavor—it was a social justice mission. But such bold pursuits came at a cost. Amidst the recognition and acclaim, there were dark undertones—ominous death threats and a period where he had to live covertly, to step ahead of potential dangers.

Yet, even under such pressing circumstances, he demonstrated the essence of a Challenger. Instead of retreating, he used these

TYPE 8—STRENGTH

threats as a catalyst, furthering his dedication to expose hidden injustice and empower the next generation of activists.

To me, he was more than a professor—he was a beacon of strength, illuminating the path of fierce determination and integrity. Through his journey, Professor Jones taught us that true leadership is not just about assuming authority, but about wielding it with purpose and heart.

Professor Jones' story offers a striking glimpse into the core of Type 8 dynamics. Let's delve deeper and unpack all the traits that make up this resilient archetype.

PERSONALITY TRAITS OF TYPE 8

Desire: To Protect and Empower

At the core of your personality lies a strong need to protect and empower both yourself and those around you. In daily life, this manifests as a vigilant eye against injustice. Whether it's intervening when someone is being mistreated on the sidewalk, standing up for a colleague being unfairly treated at work, or advocating for a family member who seems overshadowed, you're there.

You have a keen sense for when power is being misused or when someone is being taken advantage of, and you don't hesitate to step in.

Yet, balance is key. This desire can sometimes manifest as an overpowering need to control, leading to conflicts. There's a line between offering support and overpowering others. It's in navigating this balance where your true empowerment lies—not just in leading, but in allowing others to find their own strength and voice.

Emotion: Intensity (Externalized Anger)

Your emotional world is defined by intense energy—your feelings run deep and strong. You feel that your value and purpose is tied to how bold and assertive you can be. Because of this, you've built a strong outer shell, protecting a soft heart that not many get to see.

But when people misunderstand your fiery energy, it feels like they're missing or misunderstanding a big part of you. Underneath it all, there's a hidden wish—for someone to see past your intensity and acknowledge the tender side of you, giving you the space to be truly vulnerable.

Fixation: Control and Challenge

Your need to protect and empower often translates into an impulse to control and challenge situations. Like confronting a colleague each time you sense an inequity, it's your way of maintaining order and ensuring fairness. While this has its merits, it can sometimes come off as confrontational or domineering.

There's a fine line between defending against injustice and unintentionally contributing to it. Your reactions, though grounded in a quest for justice, can be impulsive. This can create tension in your interactions, as your assertiveness might be perceived as overbearing or antagonistic. Effectively championing the causes you care about involves balancing your protective instincts with a trust in life to balance the scales of justice and in people's journey toward developing their own inner strength.

Shadow: Fear of Vulnerability

Beneath your formidable exterior lies a profound fear of vulnerability. This is perhaps your most closely guarded secret. While your strength and assertiveness are undeniable, they also serve as armor against perceived inner weaknesses. You believe that to show vulnerability is to invite betrayal or manipulation.

Yet, this shield, built from layers of resilience and control, isolates you. It can prevent you from experiencing the depth of connection and intimacy that comes from letting others see your genuine self, vulnerabilities and all. When faced with situations that threaten to expose this tenderness, you might double down on your strength—at the cost of deepening your relationships or personal growth.

This internal struggle defines the delicate balance between power and vulnerability in each of us.

MEET KAREN, A PROTECTOR'S JOURNEY TO VULNERABILITY

> From the moment Karen walked into my office she was a force of nature—radiating confidence and authority. At her job and in her personal life, she was the defender, the one others turned to for protection. But as we delved deeper, a paradox emerged. Karen, so adept at defending others, struggled to stand up for her own emotional needs.
>
> Karen hid a deep fear—showing her soft side, her vulnerability. We used the Enneagram of Essence to dig deeper. We focused on the universal call for protection and justice that Type 8s feel. Karen started to see it wasn't just about her battles.
>
> She was part of something bigger.
>
> This shift was a game-changer. Karen realized she didn't have to be "on" and shoulder the burden all the time. She could trust in the world's bigger sense of justice and let her guard down sometimes.
>
> One day, Karen shared an incident at work. A dispute arose, and her instinct was to intervene and take charge. However, she chose to step back, observing the situation unfold. To her surprise, her colleagues found a way to resolve the issue amicably without her direct involvement. This experience was a revelation for Karen, solidifying her belief in the power of trust in others and life itself.

With time, Karen began to balance her fierce protective nature with moments of introspection and self-care. She learned that true strength wasn't just about defending others—it was also about recognizing and honoring her own vulnerabilities and emotional needs.

Karen's journey illustrates the Type 8 facet that resides within us all. But what does this type actually feel like from within? Let's dive into the sensations and experiences of this type in your body, exploring the intricacies of both its personality and essence.

SOMATIC EXPERIENCE OF TYPE 8

Energetic Direction: Outward

Compared to the other gut types—the inward depth of your Type 1 or the centered balance of your Type 9—your Type 8 orientation turns outward, projecting your innate strength and protective energy to those around you. You actively seek opportunities to engage with assertiveness, champion justice, and foster empowerment.

For instance, if you pass someone on the sidewalk and observe they are being unfairly treated, while others may pass by passively, your Type 8 nature drives you to intervene and challenge the situation—boldly standing up for the underdog, ensuring they are protected.

In Stress: Challenging

On the outside, people feel your formidable strength, like a protective wall. People often only see this commanding exterior, unaware of the intricate undercurrents of vulnerability and tenderness swirling inside you.

Internally, your gut is like a finely-tuned instrument, constantly alert to the subtleties in your environment. It's as if every nerve is hyper-aware, helping you swiftly distinguish between allies and adversaries. This heightened sensitivity is your radar, guiding your interactions and decisions.

Even when you seem relaxed, there's a palpable tension in your body—your muscles, especially around your shoulders and jaw, are often taut, ready for action. This physical readiness is a manifestation of your energetic preparedness to face challenges head-on. Deep within, beneath the layers of resilience and assertiveness, lies a seldom-seen tenderness—a genuine nurturance and vulnerability that you guard fiercely. This hidden aspect of your being holds the key to a more balanced and fulfilling existence, where strength and softness coexist.

With Essence: Embodied Power

When survival mode recedes, you embody a deep, centered power. Internally, you feel an expansive warmth, a joy that knows no bounds. Your gut, once constantly vigilant, now rests in calm receptiveness. The warmth in your chest expands, creating connection through vulnerability. The tension in your shoulders and jaw eases, giving way to relaxed confidence.

This grounded power brings forth a sense of true justice and potential, with a touch of innate innocence. It's a presence that inspires others, inviting authentic collaboration and shared joy, demonstrating how true strength is both powerful and gentle.

Relish this empowering sensation as we move into our final section and get to know the mature Type 8.

MATURE TYPE 8 — FIXATION TO ESSENCE

Your Type 8 evolution is about expanding your inner strength to include a deeper embrace of vulnerability, freeing yourself from the need to constantly protect against injustices.

TYPE 8—STRENGTH

Imagine yourself as a mature, majestic mountain—inherently commanding and providing refuge and sanctuary to those who are drawn to you.

Remember your relentless drive to protect and empower?

It's matured into an intuitive discernment. Now, you skillfully navigate when to actively step in and when to take a step back, offering support and trust in others' capacity to stand up for themselves. This balance allows you to advocate effectively without overshadowing, fostering empowerment in a way that's supportive yet not dominating.

Your relationships have evolved, too. They've deepened and flourished, enriched by your recognition and acceptance of your own vulnerabilities. This shift has allowed you to forge more genuine, understanding connections. The people in your life now see a more introspective and empathetic side of you, leading to stronger, more meaningful bonds. They appreciate the new depth of tenderness in your interactions, finding comfort and joy in your willingness to lean on them and share your softer side. This mutual exchange of vulnerability and strength brings a refreshing, fulfilling dynamic to your relationships.

And, what about your need to push boundaries?

It has matured into a conscious choice aligned with true empowerment. You no longer challenge for the sake of asserting your power and shielding your weakness. You know that showing vulnerability enhances your strength. Now, your boundary-pushing comes from a place of thoughtful consideration, balancing the need to stand firm with the grace of empathy and understanding. This nuanced approach allows you to advocate more effectively, understanding when to assertively step forward and when to allow space for others to grow.

It's a remarkable transformation, can you envision it?

You're still you though, embodying your natural assertiveness, but now it's fueled by a balanced inner strength rather than a reactive need to control or confront. Your ability to embrace your anger and your tenderness constructively is a true mark of your maturity and inner power.

With that, I'll conclude this chapter by revisiting my story about how my instinct to protect overshadowed the sensitivity and support my friend truly needed. Here's how it unfolded.

AND SO, I FOUND MYSELF AT A CROSSROADS

After my friend was wronged, my world shifted dramatically. Every fiber of my being screamed for justice, consumed by a desire to right the profound wrong that had deeply affected my friend. My heart was full of anger towards the person responsible, pulsing with thoughts of revenge. This battle felt deeply personal, echoing the fixated aspects of my Type 8 energy.

In this storm of emotions—ranging from fierce protectiveness to rage—I envisioned confrontations that would set the world right. But in my pursuit of justice, I lost sight of the person who needed me most—my friend.

She needed healing and solace, while I was distant, engulfed in my own need for justice. The realization struck too late. Weeks passed, and as my plans for justice dissolved, I found myself alone, my dear friend gone. In a long period of solitude, I discovered the true cost of my actions—or rather, my inactions.

My friend had needed me as a companion on her journey back from pain. She needed the version of me that could listen, offer

TYPE 8—STRENGTH

a shoulder, and be a source of comfort, but I am grateful she found the connection she needed elsewhere.

After a long while, when I attempted to reconnect and repair the bond, I faced the painful reality that our friendship had irreparably diminished. I had missed the chance to be the support she truly needed, leaving me with regret and a yearning for what no longer was. This chapter of my life taught me an invaluable lesson about the essence of Type 8—it embodies not only the roar but also the whisper, the capacity for empathy and gentle presence in times of pain.

This profound experience has instilled in me a deep sense of gratitude and growth. I have come to cherish the lessons taught by my inner Type 8, embracing both its formidable strength and its capacity for vulnerability. This journey has underscored the importance of truly listening and being present for others, not just in moments of crisis but across all aspects of life. It's a lesson that has profoundly shaped my approach to relationships.

Thank you for accompanying me on this intense journey. I hope my stories and insights have ignited deeper introspection within you.

Next, you'll find practical steps for embodying your Type 8 essence, designed to help you move beyond limiting personality traits and integrate this wisdom into your daily life. These resources are an *introduction* to the embodiment path — setting the stage for deeper explorations available in our Essence Embodiment Certification.

For a FREE printable copy of this embodiment guide for all 9 types, please visit my website: EnneagramofEssence.com

EMBODIMENT
PATH TO STRENGTH
EMBRACING TYPE 8 ESSENCE

JOURNEY INTO ESSENCE
The Enneagram of Essence's practical power is rooted in embodying essence and releasing limiting patterns. This brief guide to embodying Type 8's empowerment is my gift, setting the stage for a much deeper exploration available in my full programs.

STRENGTH THROUGH TYPE 8 ESSENCE
Even though Type 8 is not my primary type, its essence energizes me with strength and vitality. *How could Type 8 essence enrich your inner and outer world?*

NATURE'S JUSTICE
Imagine standing before a vast canyon, feeling humbled yet empowered by it's immensity. This is Type 8's robust spirit.

MIND-BODY WELLNESS
Studies in psychophysiology show that recognizing and harnessing your intrinsic power fosters deep resilience, creating the foundation for a life filled with empowerment.

© 2023 Enneagram of Essence. All rights reserved.

TYPE 8—STRENGTH

> **EMBODIMENT**
> # Path to Strength
> **EMBRACING TYPE 8 ESSENCE**

Step 1: Identify Portals To Strength

Identify what ignites feelings of inner strength for you — nature, memories, empowered people, etc. For me, envisioning a roaring waterfall inspires a potent sense of potentiality within.

What symbols or experiences spark empowerment and inner justice for you?

Incorporate elements like colors, textures, flavors, scents and sounds that mirror this quality into your space, as reminders of your Type 8 journey.

Step 2: Feel and Anchor Strength

Notice the distinct way power and justice feel within you. When I connect with this essence, I feel a charged yet grounded energy, as if connected to the potent energy of the earth.

What does true power feel like in your body?

Practice feeling and anchoring strength deeply throughout your nervous system — visualize and feel it flow through you, influencing your posture, movements, and perceptions.

© 2023 Enneagram of Essence. All rights reserved.

Embodiment
Path to Strength
Embracing Type 8 Essence

Step 3: Center Strength

Make an effort to notice and value the energy of strength and justice in people around you. Focus on essence when noticing someone's personality.

Think about how centering this essence could change your understanding and appreciation of people with the primary Type 8.

How could this practice deepen your understanding and connections with people primarily identified as Type 8?

Step 4: Create a Practice

Incorporate these steps into a flexible and creative practice, bringing it into your daily routine from a week to a month. Focus on portals that ignite inner strength and justice. Through regular engagement, embodying true empowerment will become more and more effortless.

How will integrating these practices transform your daily life?

© 2023 Enneagram of Essence. All rights reserved.

TYPE 8—STRENGTH

EMBODIMENT
PATH TO STRENGTH
EMBRACING TYPE 8 ESSENCE

STEP 5: ABSTAIN FROM LIMITING TRAITS

Make space within yourself to cultivate empowerment. Type 8 personality traits serve as survival mechanisms so it's important to release them gently, leaning on inner resources for support.

Mindfully identify and release Type 8 patterns that detract from your essence, including:

NEGLECTING VULNERABILITIES
Embrace your vulnerability as a strength. Ground in resilience that includes tenderness.

SEEKING CONTROL
Practice accepting life's unpredictability, cultivate an *adaptable* strength, flowing with life.

DOMINANT LEADING
Lead to inspire, not intimidate. Let symbols of humble leadership guide you to empower others.

AVOIDING REFLECTION
Make time for introspection, visualize serene power, like a lion in repose — might with calm.

© 2023 Enneagram of Essence. All rights reserved.

EMBODIMENT
PATH TO STRENGTH
EMBRACING TYPE 8 ESSENCE

Step 5: Abstain from Limiting Traits
Mindfully identify and release Type 8 patterns that detract from your essence, including:

Abrupt Communication
Cultivate patience in dialogue, draw inspiration from the calm yet focused presence of an eagle.

Excessive Self-Reliance
Open up to the strength in asking for help, acknowledge others' reliability and strength.

Intimidation for Respect
Recognize and release intimidation, build connections rooted in empathy and respect.

Seeing Vulnerability as Weakness
Practice viewing vulnerability as a form of bravery — openness as a sign of inner strength.

Over-identifying with the "Protector"
Balance your protector role with your own needs, use practices that balance power dynamics.

Downplaying Sensitivities
Honor your emotional depth, develop practices that encourage openness and authenticity.

© 2023 Enneagram of Essence. All rights reserved.

Embodiment
Path to Strength
Embracing Type 8 Essence

Step 5: Abstain from Limiting Traits
Mindfully identify and release Type 8 patterns that detract from your essence, including:

Quick Reactions
Practice pausing to respond thoughtfully, using grounding symbols to foster mindfulness.

Responsibility for Justice
Share the pursuit of justice, carrying symbols that remind you of the collective effort required.

Pushing Boundaries
Discern the times to challenge limits and when to maintain them, honor respectful strength.

Black-and-White Thinking
Embrace complexity and the rich spectrum of life.

Use Step 5 as a bridge, not fixed rules. By centering essence, your personality traits will naturally relax into the nourishing qualities of inner strength, justice and empowerment.

Let's conclude with a moment of integration with this guided meditation into inner strength.

© 2023 Enneagram of Essence. All rights reserved.

GUIDED MEDITATION FOR TYPE 8

I encourage you to find a comfortable position, relax your body, and gently soften your focus. Read this slowly and with ease, twice—first to visualize the imagery, and then again to deeply connect with the sensations it evokes.

Relax your eyes.
Take in a deep, empowering breath.

You are standing on a grand mountain.
Feel the solid rock beneath your feet.

Feel the cool, brisk wind,
brushing against your skin,
refreshing and invigorating.

Inhale deeply.
Exhale with strength.
Feel a surge of power
from your core.

Above, the sky stretches endlessly,
Mirroring your vast potential.

Below, the world sprawls out,
a canvas awaiting your just touch.

Feel the steady rhythm
of life pulsing around you.

© 2023 Enneagram of Essence. All rights reserved.

TYPE 8—STRENGTH

GUIDED MEDITATION FOR TYPE 8

Listen . . .
Hear the subtle sound of nature,
the gentle murmur of the wind,
the whisper of leaves.

In the distance,
Thunder rumbles—
bold, pure, and resonant.

Take in the scent of fresh mountain air,
crisp, clean, filled with the earth's raw energy.

Above, an eagle soars—
eyes sharp, focus unwavering.

Its powerful wings beat,
resonating with natural strength.

Watch its flight—
clear, determined.
Its essence,
a mirror of your inner force.

Breathe in,
absorb strength.
Breathe out,
radiate justice.

© 2023 Enneagram of Essence. All rights reserved.

GUIDED MEDITATION FOR TYPE 8

You are not just on this mountain.
You embody its enduring power and integrity.

Pause for a moment.

How did that meditation feel? Could you sense the strength of the eagle soaring over the mountain?

If this meditation resonated with you, it's because you connected with an essential sense of power and justice that transcends situations. The imagery of the commanding mountain and the steadfast eagle serves as a gateway. However, it's crucial to remember that true power and justice are inherent, internal parts of you.

When you're ready, the next page offers closing reflections and next steps for our shared journey. May you continue to embrace the essence of universal wholeness living within you.

© 2023 Enneagram of Essence. All rights reserved.

INTEGRATION

HARVESTING YOUR POTENTIAL

This has been a profound and intimate journey through your whole being—awakening your essence and embracing your wholeness. Through each chapter, you delved into a different facet of yourself, compassionately honoring who you have been and nurturing the wholeness you are returning to.

This holistic approach transcends self-analysis, fostering a deeper somatic connection to our collective human experience. It's about acknowledging our shared fixations and strengths, seeing the common threads that unite us all.

I've shared my journey transparently, hoping it would resonate with your experiences and inspire you to reflect deeply. As you continue to navigate the ebbs and flows of life, remember that each Enneagram type lives within you in some form. Each time you encounter a challenging trait or a moment of essence, pause and explore which facet of the Enneagram is at play.

Remember, this book is a gateway, not an endpoint. It's a living guide that grows with you. Your relationship with the Enneagram will evolve as you do, continually offering fresh perspectives and deeper insights. As you move forward, let this book be an on-going companion, a source of wisdom and nurturance as you continue to explore the depths of your essence and step into the fullness of your potential.

THIS BOOK WAS DEDICATED TO YOU

You are a part of the Enneagram's evolving journey. By embracing your wholeness and essence, you contribute to a new era of understanding—a transition from fragmented notions of self to a unified, holistic perspective. We're leaving behind the days when we limited ourselves to narrow nicknames and isolated traits.

This nurtured approach to the Enneagram marks a profound maturity. We're not just bridging gaps within ourselves but also within our vibrant community. This journey moves beyond personality typing—celebrating the rich tapestry of our shared human experience. The Enneagram is more than a system of labels—it's a pathway to embracing the full spectrum of our nourished potential.

So, as you turn the final page, take a moment to pause and ponder your role in this collective experience.

AN INVITATION

Your insights are important to this dynamic, ever-growing model. Whether you choose to share these teachings formally or informally, with a friend or in a workshop, I encourage you to do so with a focus on wholeness and essence.

- How will you integrate and share this wisdom in your life?
- In what ways can you contribute to the continuous growth and maturity of the Enneagram?

Let the wisdom of the Enneagram guide you toward a deeper sense of unity and connection with yourself and others. Be a part of the Enneagram community that honors wholeness and the nourishing essence of our universal nature. It's your turn to be a guiding light of comprehension and compassion, brightening the path for others as they explore their path to self-awareness and comprehensive growth.

NEXT STEPS

It's time to turn the insights you've gathered into meaningful action. The essence of the Enneagram is not in the understanding but in the active integration of its nourishment. I invite you to nurture the roots you've laid with some of these opportunities.

Fundamentals Course

Deepen your Enneagram Essence journey with our Fundamentals Course — a 3.5-hour high-quality learning experience that also opens access to our learning community — discussion forum, monthly live groups, workshops, podcasts, and a resource library full of recorded content.

EnneagramofEssence.com/Course

Accredited Certification

'Full Circle — 9 Types in 9 Months' is an accredited Enneagram certification that centers the *essence* of each type, offering a path to growth grounded in science with our Essence Embodiment Modality.

More than just a certification, this is a movement that embraces the Enneagram's essence for deep nourishment and celebrates it as a path to wholeness.

EnneagramofEssence.com/Full-Certification

Learning Community

Join our vibrant community of Enneagram enthusiasts! Here, you can share experiences, learn from others, and connect with like-minded individuals on similar journeys:

Enneagram-of-Essence.mn.co

YouTube Channel

For ongoing essence embodiment insights that are both fun and insightful, be sure to follow Tammy's YouTube channel:

YouTube.com/@EnneagramEssence

Thank you for joining me on this journey.
Tammy

ACKNOWLEDGMENTS

TO MY HAVEN, BEN

Words fall short in capturing how deeply grateful I am to you. Your patience during those seemingly never-ending hours of writing, your keen insights as my trusted reader, and your heartfelt encouragement every step of the way have been the lifeline of this project. Not to mention the countless times you swept our kids into adventures, providing me those serene spaces to craft these pages.

TO MY WRITING COACH, WENDY VAN DE POLL

You've been **SO** much more than a writing coach to me. From our shared moments in the Enneagram of Essence training program to the inspiration you gave me to embark on this literary journey, your influence has been profound. Your wisdom, resources, and guidance were invaluable, but it was your boundless enthusiasm and unwavering faith in this book that truly ignited my spirit. I'm eternally grateful for your presence and encouragement.

TO MY EDITOR, NANCY PILE

You have a magic touch. Your reassurances gave me confidence, and your astute insights pinpointed the exact places where strengthening was needed. Your expertise brought out the best in this book, and I feel truly blessed to have had you by my side.

TO THE INSPIRATIONS BEHIND MY CASE STUDIES, MY CLIENTS AND FRIENDS

Your experiences brought depth to each type depiction. Thank you for allowing me to share snippets of your stories and for being such rich sources of understanding and learning. Your experiences have been instrumental in elucidating the depth and nuances of each type.

TO MY GENEROUS BETA READERS

Your generosity in sharing your time and insights without any expectations has enriched this book in ways I couldn't have imagined. Your varied perspectives and candid feedback have been priceless.

TO MY BELOVED LITTLES, ELI & OLI

Should you one day hold this book in your hands and remember that year when mama was engrossed with her writing, please know that my love for you resonated in each word. I deeply appreciate and cherish the moments you granted me to pursue this passion.

TO MY ENNEAGRAM BEACON, MY MOTHER

A big heartfelt thank you to my mother, whose wisdom first guided me on this path. Her visionary spirit and profound understanding of the Enneagram's depths have been a constant source of inspiration. This book is a tribute to her influence and the enthusiasm she passed on to me.

With so much love and gratitude,
Tammy

ABOUT THE AUTHOR

Tammy Hendrix, LCSW is an International Enneagram Association accredited author and clinical psychotherapist. She founded the Enneagram of Essence® to create programs that deeply explore essence and wholeness.

Her training uniquely integrates somatic, psychodynamic and Jungian therapies with introspective practices like meditation and yoga, offering a comprehensive and holistic experience in understanding and applying the wisdom of the Enneagram.

She is always cultivating new offerings and deeper paths to discover, stay tuned!

A REQUEST

YOUR VOICE MATTERS

Thank you for joining me through the pages of this book. I hope it has offered you valuable insights and a deeper, more embodied understanding of the Enneagram.

If you've found resonance and enrichment within these chapters, I warmly invite you to share your experience through a review on Amazon. Whether your reflections are brief or detailed, they contribute to spreading the essence and wisdom of the Enneagram.

Leaving a review is simple:

1. Visit the book's page on Amazon.
2. Scroll to the 'Customer Reviews' section.
3. Click 'Write a customer review.

Your voice is significant in this ongoing conversation about embracing wholeness. Thank you for taking the time to share it.

With heartfelt gratitude,

Tammy

Made in the USA
Las Vegas, NV
21 May 2024